If ignorance   is innocence

all is true   all is false

alibi has no fulcrum

Ahsahta Press
The New Series

#68

Boise, Idaho
2015

Trafficke

Susan Tichy

Ahsahta Press, Boise State University, Boise, Idaho 83725-1525

ahsahtapress.org

Cover design by Quemadura / Book design by Janet Holmes
Cover photo by Susan Tichy.

LIBRARY OF CONGRESS CATALOGING-IN-PUBLICATION DATA

Tichy, Susan, 1952–
[Poems. Selections]
Trafficke / Susan Tichy.
pages ; cm.—(The new series ; #68)
ISBN 978-1-934103-60-9 (pbk. : alk. paper)—ISBN 1-934103-60-8 (pbk. : alk. paper)
I. Title.
PS3570.I26A6 2015
811'.54—dc23
2014043598

ACKNOWLEDGMENTS

This book was written twice—once in the 1990s and again after 2010. I am deeply grateful to editors who published any portion of *Trafficke*, in any draft, including: *Indiana Review* (1999), *Phoebe* (1999), *Quarter After Eight* (1999), *Green Mountains Review* (2000), *The Literary Review* (2000), *Denver Quarterly* (2002), *Colorado Review* (2011), *Evening Will Come* (2013), *Seneca Review* (2014), *Quiddity: An International Journal of Literature and Art* (2014), and *Apartment* (2015).

Acknowledgments continue on page 178

For my mother & grandmother

Margaret Bubb Tichy
Elizabeth Cummins Magruder Bubb

in loving memory

And for Lesley Smith, *Trafficke*'s most constant companion

Contents

Anent

Literate 500 years
For me there is no New World

coir' a' chlaidheamh, milord
broomrape   reddendum   recite

Or scratch, hide, seek
erase-sketch-bird-invent

This forest, mine   this noise
I tracked until it turned and showed its teeth

ransack   deceive   predator
in the narrow passes

Thirty-one miles of metal shelves
hill path   in

•

To furthest reach   loved earth
in slow foothold

   What's that upon your back
Quo the fause knicht upon the road
   My bannoch and my books
Quo the wee child—rash exactitude

of ballad method, wayward wood
(or stumble, blackmail, stand, deliver, nil)

Has grass sprung back since stepped on, has

Unutterable   that sky consent

Eat bannoch and keep time by the tapping branches

•

Journey across the telling of it

leaves in the forest, one   then two
foam on the river   troublesome

Power line follows the drove road
real serpent wrapped around the abstract Z

that is or isn't   *seanachie*
a genealogical perjury

Scroll terminates in leaves or flowers
thicket   radiance   ridge   *ri*

a phyllomorphic posturing
illegible by attrition, or

Gospel of presence   acreage
appears in the interstices

damaging parchment   numerous holes
where what revealed   is bowered

'S rioghail mo dhream—royal my blood—
as granite spills from the rivers

come   misgive

& Anent

I was born and raised in Maryland, an eleventh generation immigrant. My maternal grandmother's maiden name, Magruder, went back to the 1650s, when one Alexander McGruder, of Perthshire, Scotland, arrived as a transported prisoner of war. (How many kids in my grade school had heard of Oliver Cromwell?) And there was more. As *Magruders* we were also *MacGregors*—Highlanders—with a flashy red tartan, some great pipe tunes, and a long, tortuous, violent history, of which we were taught to be proud, never mind the details. I don't remember being told the clan stories; neither do I remember not knowing them. At seven, I was given my first potted history of Clan Gregor—a pocket-sized book still sold on Edinburgh's Royal Mile—and hunted through it for answers to questions I was already asking.

About Alexander, himself, my sources—by which I mean my mother and grandmother—were strangely vague: as targets of genocide, MacGregors had been forced to change their names, and Alexander's family must have done so. Or maybe the Magruders were a *sept* or division within the clan. Maybe some early Maryland clerk just misheard, or couldn't spell, *MacGregor*. But whatever the story, we were ready to defend it, for to be a MacGregor—and *still* a MacGregor despite three hundred years and the small matter of a large ocean—was an act of resistance, a badge of survival. Like saying *I am Apache. Piscataway. Jew.* In fact, it was while reading the history of another holocaust—the nine-tenths reduction in population suffered by Natives in the Chesapeake after European contact—that I first began to see Alexander Magruder as an historical person, not a legendary one, for he was, after all, one of the first arrivants. Who was he? *What* was he? What was *Maryland*?

These questions made me aware of another silence: the three hundred years, exactly, between Alexander's landing and my birth; a silence so clamorous and spooky that I was past forty before I dared admit I didn't actually know where in Maryland my ancestors had lived. Trying to picture it, I saw my own hand holding something like a jigsaw piece, unable to find a place on the map to set it down. It wasn't from the county where I grew up, and it didn't fit in the western mountains; nor in Baltimore; nor on the Eastern Shore. For a while, my hand hovered over the Chesapeake Bay, but no lost continent rose up to deliver me. The only place left was Southern Maryland, the slave-owning tobacco country lying between the bay and the Potomac, a part of the state my parents never spoke of without scorn.

Silence is the domain of language, as certainly as unfilled space defines the design, even the legibility, of a page.

·

Then will ye tak the gun, the gun
Or will ye tak the arrow
Or will ye tak the gey broadsword

Ransack   misgive   the border

Night Orders

Night orders are not good, and these were mine: ane sword and oak tree cros-sit beneath ane crowne. The versions differ only slightly—same rhymes, same *punctilios*. An act of faith, or fiction: inheritance through the male. Possession inscribed in the *Ri Albain, Chronicle of the Scots, Chronicle of the Picts and Scots.* In martyrdom red, white, or green. In gospel books, *scriptoria,* in St. Adomnán's Law. Or, in a bedtime story, of Clan Landless, Nameless. *Not good to be of ill-famed race. Not good to neglect the dogs.* Hounds interlace like ribbons down the edge of an empty page, whose absent gospel shapes the tale

of great iron fetters for men's feet
of small iron fetters for men's hands

Heroic figure slips to the margin, vanishes into the hounds and knotwork. Dare interpret, dare apprentice, say: *grotesque human form in clasp of a dragon,* or *obviously a Holy figure, great combat and an ink pot attached to the end of a stick*— Illuminator's puzzle book, made for one who already knows it by heart.

Now the adder lies in the corbie's nest

deliberate avoidance of real resemblance
troublesome curve of the nose   if

Presence of self on the long path
inner map of resistance   daily drawn

who can become   by words archaic
outlawed   a plenitude

(your ear maun be the only judge
quaintly advised to purchase
or hang on the Black Crucifix)

Now fornication   unruly birth
of leaf in April elegance
all made over to new accounts—

cherished page in a comfortable room
climate-controlled artistry
she stands by a window   he turns on a path
well-marked by narrative
by bedtime story   hero of first
permanently susceptible
to the romance of the perishing

(young man on a garron
dun horse of the Gael
some kind of escape   or wakening)

Get ye doun frae ma horse, you're a brazen-faced whour

Walk sunwise   complex with craft
a suffering

Something my mother told me: kinship is vertical, a trellis of writing, pruned and trained, with white spaces, mended. By which wife? *Margaret? Sarah? Elizabeth?* A question-mark is a thing of beauty: my mother's pencil all through the margins. Her handwriting appears at every exit, crosses through sentences, alters names. Bodies spiraling round and down, filled in, crossed out, corrected. To a *fair copy*, stylized tale, its decorative border of monsters redesigned. By this we prove possession. Great quantities of land, a name. Or mystery eponymous, a danger to the telling of it, beast allowed to perish. In that *deer-trap, funnel-shaped defile* of pen and paper, rhyme and spelling, noisy dispute of the territory. *The whole country is a perfect forest*, a few plantations cleared to my hand. *Child with a streak of milk on one cheek, a streak of blood on the other*. Cleared by whom?

Then go ye up unto this feast
thirled to repetition   O my heart

Theory of tyranny under attack
manuscript poem by someone missing

The river rises to the Red Cross tents
unsolved in a sacred text

one unsigned page in my mother's drawer
—typescript on onionskin—
three fugitive opinions I purchased in Australia
—internet search for the last copy—
oak tree on the coat of arms
—the gallows—

2

In Clan Gregor history there is one great fact: their *Proscription*, in 1603, by the newly minted James I—lately King James VI of Scotland. His first official act, some say, born of a need for order in the *peccant* parts of his realm.

> **Proscribe** *vb tr* [ME *proscriben*, fr L *proscribere*, to publish in
> writing: (15c) 1: to denounce or condemn 3: (Obsolete) to pub-
> lish the name of (a person) as outlawed [IE *skeri-* to cut, separate,
> sift 1b: L *scribere* 1c: GR *skariphos* 2: OE *hridder*, sieve, riddle]

He directed, in London, two score learnéd and pious men to translate the Bible into their native tongue. He directed, in Scotland, that all good subjects commence at once to *extirpate Clan Gregor and to ruit oot their posteritie and name*. Pardon only by self-annihilation: the name *MacGregor* was henceforth annulled. All who bore it must renounce it, scatter among the other clans—as Murray, Stewart, Campbell, Grant, McNab. No signature of the name was legal, no contract so signed was binding. Children of fourteen were hanged. And women were hunted the same as men, *to slauchter and mutilate them*, and to raise fyre. Wives who stood by their husbands were branded on their foreheads, transported to the Lowlands, to Ireland, Barbados—I don't know—to Vanishment—while any who slew a MacGregor shared his property with the crown. Warrants to hunt this *wickit and rebellious clan* could be purchased, as for any dangerous beast.

> teacher who bade me speak of myself, I do
> this horrifying tenancy
> archive where the only light is on the stairs

beast fable
(mediated)
humanized by what it will defend

And what brought about this *marvelous hunt*? Ask a MacGregor—ask my moth-
er—she'd say politics and betrayal, the greed of barons, the theft of land. And
not far to look for an arch-villain: Clan Campbell's ambition to rule—if not all of
Scotland at least every inch of it they could put their foot on. *Clan Campbell grew
by the way of the wild ash*, a Highland proverb says of them: a tree straight and
fair that kills all living things within its shadow. But ask a Campbell, he'll point
to the Records of the Privy Council, where *mocking, mayhem, and murder* march
closely with Clan Gregor's name. So, who had voice at the Privy Council, and who
did not? It was never an equal contest—wealth and power against the cult of
honor and a strong sword arm. The old pipe tunes express our neighborly ways:
The Burning of the Black Mill, Lifting the Cattle, The Fallen Chief. Even the *Reel of
Tulloch* composed by a happy fugitive, who had killed every man of a band who
came against him.

but wolves and wilde boares who spoil at blood
be not too long at a tune

for covering harps, the skulls are many
given us by these fierce hounds

Glen Fruin was the final straw—Glen of Sorrows—where, in a February bog land,
two or three or four hundred MacGregors met eight hundred sent to annihilate
them—and had the great temerity to rout them. Eighty dead, or one hundred
forty: only two MacGregors.

—

10

Ploughing by night what I think is true
—not clever enough to burn the evidence—
black undulation   shadowed hill
where a yew tree grows at the altar

And lyke as the clude discendis frome the air
make welcome, m'Lord   an history
caesarian delivery   at swordpoint into snow

Landless!—that weepy refrain of Sir Walter Scott's faux Clan Gregor anthem, with
its catalogue of lost glens and castles: Glen Orchy, Glen Lyon, Kilchurn, Glen
Strae. It translates—as any Maryland tobacco planter could tell you—as *power-
less*. But those Clan Gregor ancestors were no unlanded laborers, willing to *bend
back and knee* just to earn their bread. Unable to farm, they lifted cattle by the
score and hundred. Barred recourse to law, they fell back on that old reliable, *coir'
a' chlaidheamh*—right of the sword—coming sometimes in such arrogant strength
as to sell their *spreighs* openly on the Lowland markets.

a fierce-looking fellow and his eyes are grey
he is fond of talk, a great Rogue
and when drunk stammers in his speech
she is cunning and artful, may change her name
And the unborn in the womb

Cuckoo and ring dove, brown stag at morning
he who brings me kisses and a full branch
my kertch from Dunkeld, my belt from Edinburgh
my gloves with gold tips to the fingers

—So say the songs, of truth ineligible

For those old MacGregors, by *sturt and strife,* were efficient wielders of ravagement. Hunters to the end, they never did learn to keep still, like prey. Fornicators and murderers. Suspicious, vengeful, insolent: you would not like them. I know I don't (for I can doubt while believing). What made them so hard? My mother said *pride,* said *family.* Said *she's be burnt and he's be slain.* Fact says long tenure as shock troops, a personal army, to the very Campbell lords who now pursued them. It was, you could say, a falling out among thieves.

Eagle and osprey   little roe deer
what might be a glance between them
and the rock

Which rock?   All of it
one thousand years of city at my feet
smoke-dark or sand-blasted
years thousand one rewriting
same-small-space

Hanged on a black, blasphemous cross at the west end of St. Giles

Now piper in a black sweater
slow pibroch   rain in his hair
In coloured glass, dark from this side
grace recedes   elaborately
Rain in his long, lovely hair
And elsewhere

It was real enough, the genocide. But so, too, is the backstory, the shape-shift from oppressor to oppressed. So before *thee deidlie feud of the clangregoure*; before the landrent called McTarlich's Band, wherein Black Duncan Campbell of Glenurchy gave lifetime lease *and to their heirs* to the brothers McTarlich, to be paid not in crops nor goods nor ewes, but in MacGregor blood, *spilled baith privilie and oppenlie*; before Marion Campbell of Glen Lyon fell in love with the young chief, Gregor MacGregor of Glenstrae; before he was *untopped* by her kinsmen; before their son led the clan to catastrophic victory at Glen Fruin—we must take stock of the long, uproarious party: one hundred and fifty years in which MacGregors and their feudal masters—the Glen Orchy Campbells—were boon companions, fighting and *conquessing* their way from Kilchurn in the west, eastward along Glen Dochart and down Glen Lyon, all the way through Fortingall and Dull, to a pair of castles—one Campbell and one MacGregor—at Balloch, the foot of Loch Tay; adding land and castles, churches and poets, even libraries to their sphere: the Lordship of Breadalbane, which neither clan could have held without the other.

Honor requires obstinacy
right down to the last misspelling

Say difficult without it, say
to publish scarifies   creates

craig   cnoc   coire   weem

They took their style from their territory
of which transcribe   the riddle

Pleasing to witness hounds pursue
(old, certain, swift-footed tale)

but fyre in thatch   I say
is a disproportion
woman is something birth corners
black-homeless-drunken-alphabet
crouched in fertilized egg as the home burns

O Mother Mary, may grace be doubled for them, who for six generations did what they did. Blood and rain. Dirty handful of raw oats. Elegant shrug. Of which we say: *proud and too brave, never behind where a fight was offered, never forgetting a friend.* A typological headache. Ask anyone: *the hills, Clan Gregor, and the Devil came into the world at the same time.*

And how, then   shriven

To putt down innosent men, to cause
pure bairnes and inffantis bege
and pure women to perisch for hunger
quhen they are heirit of their geir

Oh yes, these

Punctilios of genealogy
otherwise devoured by the gallows

Confess I have used the same libertie of feete
Fashioned and reduced unto a method

November in Glen Lyon: a flat tire on the rental car, which, earlier, I had backed over a heap of stones. *Fionn had twelve castles in the crooked glen of the stones,* and today we have found one I missed on earlier visits: Carnbane, White Swan, on a steep knoll north of the narrow road. Present though unseen, Fionn's castle may be one of the mounds we clambered over, roped to the present by the roots of rowan and sycamore. The standing ruins are a Campbell stronghold: firing slits survive in the red stone walls. Here was born Marion Campbell, whose marriage to Gregor MacGregor of Glenstrae failed to heal the feud between their families. *They laid his head on an oaken block / and there let fall his blood,* she wrote. *And had I a cup I'd have drunk my fill.* Verse composed not in *the small art* of woman's song, but the *tall verse* of castle and hall: "Griogal Cridhe," Beloved Gregor, lament and lullaby in one. No need to explain it to my friend, because three days ago we heard Margaret Bennett sing it, in Edinburgh. But now we are in tall woods at the Pass of Lyon, narrowest point of the glen, our car barely off the right-of-way, and the short northern light is waning. There's no spare tire, and we've seen only four or five cars all day, so we walk down the road to the first habitation, a row of thatched cottages my map says must be Artrasgairt. One looks inhabited, modernized. We knock on the door and are taken in, led through. *Yes, here is the phone. I'll make some tea. And from America, really? What brings you up here at this time of year?* At the back of the house, a cluttered conservatory, space-heater humming in the winter light. Poetry books lie open on the table.

3

And Alexander? We said he was *MacGregor* by another name, an officer of some sort in the Royalist army—unlikely occupation for an outlawed man. Transported by Cromwell, he survived indenture, purchased land. He may or may not have married a woman who may or may not have existed—Margaret Brathwaite, daughter of a cousin of Lord Baltimore. And two more women after her—Sarah and Elizabeth, maiden names debated. His children *lived*, most of them, in a time when most did not. To this, many thousands could testify, our family lines kept as jealously as the pedigrees of deerhounds. But of Alexander himself we knew as little as we knew of Kenneth mac Alpin, the medieval king—of what was, at that time, almost Scotland—from whom we were said to descend.

a highway laid
from battlement

mountain and mountain and water
imperishable

There *was* a King Alpin—it being a common Pictish name, Son of the Hills. *He was slain in Galloway after he laid it waste*— Or was that his uncle? *Very few and lame are the documents,* but splendid the orthography.

eight parchment leaves
on the last of which

we enter this story where the rats leave off

But I remember the high tale
ancient antique edgeless dudgeon, or

white line down the center of a high-speed road

Sun and mist on the thighs of hills
stone fence reveals the curvature
(fast horses, good food)
till wrath wakes   red-cheeked

Puir pepelis, the inhabitaris—
the land is ours   if we can find it
in dimestore biographies
cheap editions of scholarly tomes
where bees make honey in a cow's ribcage
the fear of poets audible   and sweet

(add three notes to each bar   misspell the figure
leaving unintelligible sky)

·

Then what rhythm is asking?
Night stand   a battlement
if brute honor and further to cut   think

Here is the ballad   darkness balancing on tongue
one woman strays and I am not his

I am his

Harrier tilting over the meadow
she hunts by sound

churring   itinerant   remorse

Hush, child, your mother is talking to you

it's a bedtime story
it's a story about freedom
it's a bedtime story
it's a ghost

•

Then what's the blood that's on your sword?
(overly convoluted storm
that it would not be ruled by me)
Blood of my horse, my hound, my hawk

To speak truth now   unmannerly

(afterwards they have the death
tanistic and   the next rank under

it will be observed that some of the words
Annals of Ulster mention, and

———

Try to imagine a bare-assed man
heart composed   to lion

Stonechat sings on a graveyard wall
mine is not the story they tell
though tyranny of metre preserves the language

In exophoric anthem   stride
to *herskit*   or a wilding
of storm shadow   storm light
that I can desire

(if a hand is put under her clothing to her shame
if she is made pregnant by stealth)

Sound of letters rubbing together
to heart means
strike in the region of the heart
or: build up the inner sheaves

Thirty sheep in a rainstorm
and mist sweeps   delicately
across a rhyme   near-rhyme

Theirs was   effortlessly
not where stone heaves under grass   and is

New carpentry   old hinges
History begins   where it changes

Meadow

Exile   a meadow of equal

This matter of altering boundaries
whereof nine-tenths of them have died

That noe Contest may arise concerning my will

Landing places for goods
warrior counts for both sides of the river

Or, the survivor of them

Affirm that before the arrival broke out amongst them

measles   smallpox   indemnity
five hundred fishing ships a year
And lawful to trafficke

•

Now learn strength of arms, perswade myself
(as dies in hissing gore the spark)

I entered the woods and discovered nine trees in ten had been cut down
An wilderness

that you wreste no worde from his natural sounde
Let us take the forde as we find it

*

Endeavor
To examine village sites on both sides of the river

Layers impeccable
difficult to conceal less than

Courage answers   edges unworked
postmolds detected failed to yield

thousands but
complexity   dense   defied attempts

The soil of an huge and unknown greatnesse
Very well peopled and towned   though savagelie

where   it meanders

Refugium for those displaced
palisaded towns implied   confirmed
corn beans squash: the trinity

And sunlight, when it came   altogether desire
ten thousand geese on a river of pollen: spring

—
24

In Peace of Warres

1652: a forty-one year-old Scotsman arrived in the Royal Colony of Maryland. *Near Turkey Buzzard*, some say, *in the Patuxent River*. In October of the following year he appears in an indenture, by which Charles Stewart assigns to Alexander Macruder 50 acres of land. And in November, another 50 assigned by John Ashcomb to *Alexander Macruder, my servant*.

near Turkey Buzzard
what did they feast?

with litill skaith   bark and stone
content with the slaughter we do

In 1652, one chronicler says, the Atrakwaeronnons of Maryland lost 500 people carried off by the Iroquois, and unknown others killed. *Atrakwaeronnons* is a lost word, manifest yet rudderless among the named islands. Were they part of a larger people? Or some unknown, who vanished into periphery?

an harvest of wilde beaste
this luxury
appeal   to the actuary

Perhaps the Susquihanoes were Atrakwaeronnons. Perhaps; because in 1652 they signed a peace treaty with Maryland in order to turn their full wrath on the Iroquois. Perhaps; because catastrophe makes a people over in its image. For the Susquehannicks, the making was as fine as the illuminator's art: they lost half their population in five years.

> pigment of the opening words
> trumpet pattern   red lead
> or else, an extirpation

> white paint of ashes   bird bones
> the artist left blank spaces where

> death of unnaturall naturals
> *so full of indians*   or *fleet*

From 1628, four years before the founding of Maryland, William Claiborne's Protestant Company had *stood siezed* of Kent Island, in the Chesapeake Bay. Funded by Puritan backers, commissioned by the Virginia Company to explore its northern reaches, Claiborne with a hundred men traded upriver with the Susquehannocks, for thick, northern furs. The Susquehannas were Iroquoian, yet enemies of the Iroquois: a canny people, quick to ally themselves with the best of the *fighting Englishmen* at Kent.

> vortex of acquisitive violence
> at the southern edge of beaver

1632: King Charles I chartered two-thirds of the Chesapeake to George Calvert, Secretary of State to his father, James I. In a puzzle of knotwork, Calvert was, perhaps, the most intricate knot. After twenty years perfecting the diplomatic art—the compromise and the circumspect—he announced on the eve of Catholic exclusion from *any position of trust or profit,* his own conversion. Not *from,* but *to.* A man, O Lord, of principle, erupting like a discolored growth on the prominent nose of its opposite? Perhaps. For Calvert did not change parties. There was in his mind a beam of light, a divine division of politics from faith. Forced to send him from court, his king created him *Lord Baltemore,* with land in Ireland and on the shores of a continent where Englishmen aplenty had found the violent death of their imaginings. George Calvert never got that far. Dead before the Great Seal was fixed to his charter, he left to his son, Cecelius, his title, his lands, and his difficulties.

vncivill or disorderly
imprisoned as before expressed
in vested silk remembrance

oaks perfect a silence if
and shrill forest tending

to wonders and profits beyond the seas
East India Company
Virginia Company
Ireland, Newfoundland, self-defense

To beg of his king a sanctuary
a Terra MariÆ   Catholic ground
to give no offence to Protestants
to be silent upon all dispute

no cipher, no
but privily

and a *very great investment* in   restraint

Now trimming silk and sewing linen
branches against the windowsill
half of it frightened   half of it wrong

a dissident topography
where *this fals warld* is real

(Not a Southern state, my mother said
play Yankee, play)   like a blackbird
whistle and sing

Pipe tune showing through fiddle or fret
verbe too fare behind the nowne
and why then so slack?

In posturing of durst or dust
who apt to dare

A kind of beginning—one we can choose—but even the backstory has its backstory. Ships on the coast for two hundred years—Spanish and Portuguese, English and French. Finding no back door to the wealth of Asia, they settled for mapping, fishing, and a little commerce with *the naturals*. A century before Maryland was Maryland, Spanish Jesuits christened the Chesapeake Bay *Bahía de Santa Maria*. Tempted to mission, they died violently on its shores. Knives and trade beads, crosses and cloth traveled far up the tributaries. And what from the first handshake?

measles   smallpox   indemnity
but savagelie did   and prepared another
All for the clearing of a light day

Affirm   that before the arrival broke out amongst them

not *New*   but grieving
not *virgin*   but *widowed*

that whosoever believeth in Him

Five hundred fishing ships a year

And so, the Calverts: into this *wilderness*, into this fable—mediated by mattock and sword—Catholic gentlemen, Protestant servants, voyage of the *Ark* and *Dove*. St. Mary's City to be the capital: the metes and bounds of a feudal manor surveyed on the body of a sweating, malarial swamp. *An Hierarchical replica* of every English disease. Catholic worship to remain private, even in a Catholic colony.

o glorious engirdling
lovely gloom!
and a gold comb in the offering

The traders at Kent were not best pleased. Within two years, Calvert—the king's man—and Claiborne—that brave, ambitious trafficker, perennial pain in the royal ass—had, *by ill nature and worse nurture*, vowed each one to destroy the other, to *cast out words amongst the Savages,* build up fortes and settlements, and *furnish it with some murtherers.* Neither succeeded, quite; but they and their kind destroyed the Susquihanoes, Piscataways, and a long alphabet of the unaffiliated: the scattered towns and cornfields of Pawtuxent.

in Peace of Warres and Wares of Peace
a profitable excursion

doe them no favour but they will returne it
entire heart abscond

2

The people of Maryland who were not Susquehannocks, allies of Claiborne, were Algonquians, town dwellers, with hunting camps inland and oyster flats to manage the starving spring. Piscataways, along the Potomac, grouped round a paramount chief and warred where they would. But towns on the Patuxent were unpalisaded and small: no ossuaries, no kings, *and each small place sufficient*. Peace was policy, Powhatan neighbors a short trip by canoe. They traded upriver: shells for dyes, pucca for stone. And farmed. Aquintinack, Assamacomaco, Mattapanient, Yoa-comaco. Free to sell food and a village to this new set of Englishmen, who, if they survived malaria and winter, promised protection against the Susquehannahs.

(Buy stock of corne from the Naturals

(Cannot carry yourselves so toward them

(Discontentment with your habitation

(Speakers temporary or permanent
Not clearly explained in the documents)

And is it not miraculous
They should like lambes yeeld themselves
Glad of our company
Giveing us houses, land, and liveings

Less labor and so abundantly
One acre to feed for one year an humble man

And strange mortalitie
Five-eighths among the immigrants
Nine-tenths of the country people, loving and kind

Most precise example in Renaissance English
of the myth of the gentle savage

Aquintanack, Patuxent, Assamacomoco, Mattapanient

never so simple
although they signed treaties requiring

barrel-roof, smoke hole, and venerate corn
at Mattapanient   perpetuity
failed to yield a convincing house pattern

(uninterested in the afterlife)

say beastes in the shape of Men
corn fields in the shape of women   and

*

Concerneing the deer you sent for
The cedar you sent for bye him
And usefull tymber

The Lyon I had for you is dead
The beaver wch I sent you the last
Procured a red bird but had the ill fortune
Of women and children I make no estimate
Out of the sheriffes custody into my owne
They trembled to hear our ordinance
And some greate goode is meant toward these people
Their bow is but weake and shoots level but little way
Liable   Salient   Grove   Perturb
White Oake for Pipe-staves, red Oake for wainescot
The Walnut, Cedar, Pine, and Cipress
Chesnut, Elme, Popler, Ashe

Which has been cleared is thicker in woods than it was before the clearing

And peaceable, free from all scurrilous words
As temperance in eating and drinking
Their justice each to another
The English do often trust them with truck
And the rude boaring of them
Answer was made, there was held a Match-comaco
Who makes a speech unto God and want not courage
. Bid them take fire in their hands or mouthes
They live for the most part in townes
And shew no greate desire of heaping wealth
Very glad of traffick and commerce
And be feared

—

33

3

So what was Maryland? An aftermath of epidemic? The slim, hammered edge of a new idea? Or the far edge of a battlefield, contested by strange words in archaic spellings? Yes and yes: these, and more. *Poor peoples, the inhabitors*, the land is ours if we can find it. So how shall we track it, what shall we call this *mingling beast beset with foes?*

Stench of wounds in the center text
tangled lines in the knotwork

Call it *ornament*, call it *maze*
or a ship's rigging run with rats

If ignorance   is innocence
all is true   all is false
alibi has no fulcrum

Say *who*, say *what*, say *when*, say I
(amateur   drunk on the details)

Forgive me when I hop the ocean
Forgive me when I snarl the way

commerceing   heretick
speake   reproachfull

As I forgive you   the flinching

This much I can tell you: that *storms brewed in other men's worlds* broke hard and long in the Chesapeake. 1637, just five years after the Maryland charter, King Charles took a fancy to impose the Anglican liturgy on Scottish Presbyterians. Who signed a Covenant, raised an army, and invaded the English borders—all to defend their militant Kirk from the *Book of Common Prayer*. The Scots couldn't win. Neither would they go home. So in 1640, Charles called his Parliament into session, and they wouldn't go home, either. Instead, they began the revolution that would strip power from the monarchy and end in regicide. 1641 in Maryland: Jesuits defied Calvert caution, built a chapel for public worship, invited doom. 1642: a roster of battles in England, and the Sussquehannocks—roused by Claiborne, to whom they were tethered by pots and pans, Gunns Powder and shott, knives mirrors clothing and ornament—attacked the Algonquian villagers allied with Calvert, the Royalist Catholic. Birthed a decade of raids and skirmishes, spreighs and tuilzies, poison, beheading, knifing, fire.

> Asking fruit where there weren't any grew
> a plausible reason for battle
> *To row the Potomac or St. Gregory's river*
> *distributing names according to circumstances*
> Vessel abandoned to waves and wind
> it rise betimes   an effigy

1643 and a new twist: Scots Covenanters, worried by Royalist victories near their border, threw in with the English Puritans in a new pact—the *Solemn League and Covenant*, by which the English Parliament funded a Scottish army to support its own. 1643, in Maryland: Calvert's militiamen went to the Susquahannocke country, killed twenty-nine and lost but four. Or, were vanquished, lost four cannon, and fifteen Englishmen tortured to death.

So here's illumination:
a day book full of beast and bud
thogh other poets trowes ye be gone daft
On ground: fantastic pestilence
white ash unfixed to canvas where
correct translation greatly now desired
On page: a mere geometry
trumpet pattern, interlace
of *conflicts inglorious*

And how now to the battery?
Competent in the skill of conquering
well versed in *maleficium*
—that is, dealing with Satan
with Gipsies, heretics, Jews
witches and wild hielandmen—
(apples rotting in a bed of nettles)
(launching boats on the little stream)
water, earth, air, and fire
a hostile quartet for the taking

1644, in Scotland: James Graham, Marquise of Montrose—a Covenanter by religion, but a Royalist at heart—rejected the *Solemn League and Covenant*. Raised up some *wyld hielandmen*, along with some wilder *Irishes,* to defend their king and bring him, thus, into a *true* Covenant, untouched by the English stain. Defeated, after a rousing summer, by a Covenant army who massacred all prisoners. Weary historians don't lift an eyebrow, but note three hundred women and children, thrown onto the pyre of righteousness, for spice.

A knife set with gold   a palm print
    or sound of vomiting   regret

because of you, fair man
this night lie side by side

Then what's the blood that's on your sword?
my hauke sae guid
my reid-roan steid

unwashed child   striving

1645 in Maryland: *and now from the south comes gust and thunder:* one Richard Ingle, a trader aligned with Claiborne and armed with Parliament's Letter of Marque, sailed his ship, the *Reformation*, into the lower Patuxent, to *make war on Romish Tyranny*. Leonard Calvert—Lord Baltimore's brother and governor—escaped to Virginia. Ingle sent priests back to England in chains, then set sail himself, with the colony's governing gentlemen his prisoners. Left behind a ragged alliance of Protestant planters and mercenaries to plunder Catholics, Patuxents, Piscataways. Little record of this sturt and strife. *For she's be burnt and he's be slain* and those with money high-tailed it.

Puritan   Catholic   Susquehannah   Patuxent
who   owe   fidelity
two rats nibbling eucharistic bread
two pledged   to the hindering

And no dram now will drown the weather. Both shores of the ocean. Three sides, at least, to every struggle: in a mountain of books the words we need are surely in those at the bottom: a Maryland glossary, English biography, *Scottish Historical Documents,* soup of confusion, hard little facts. The occasional whole page of sense? Pinned into a timeline, like green plants hung up to dry in convenient shade.

And how goes the hunting, m'lord?

1646, in England: King Charles surrendered to the Covenanting Scots, offered to trade his throne for their right to their own Kirk: a deal. 1647: they sold him, for £200,000 the English owed them for their armies. 1648: an anti-Covenant, anti-starvation peasant uprising in Scotland. 1649: on a heath in England, landless families founded an unarmed communal farm—against the sin of property, and without reference to any earthly state. In that same year: the regicide, and the ragged launch of a second Civil War: Cromwell and his king-killing Parliament against the divided, disorganized Scots. Who purged their army leadership of all not-quite-true believers, then marched south toward defeat. At Dunbar, 1650, Worcester, 1651—surviving prisoners *Barbadoed* as fast as ships could be found to carry them. A scandal.

yet ye receive not our Witnesse
that whosoever believeth in Him

the sea rose by reason

1646 in Maryland: Leonard Calvert—returned from inglorious exile—feared for the colony. He installed a Protestant governor, then promptly died, leaving an unmarried woman executrix of his estate: a figure *most unnatural*. Yet to Maryland he bequeathed an idea even more vastly strange: to save the charter from Puritan wrath, he submitted to his new Assembly *An Act Concerning Religion*. And they, being common men, small men, afraid men—those who had, of necessity, stayed when the wealthy fled—they had the great temerity to amend it.

o god but the shame of it
egalitarian pestilence
penurious pawky pangenesis
not found on earlier maps under any name

So what had they learned in their trial by fire, these men avaricious and principled? What did they fear, as they wrote their quaint punctilios, on a tough velum, a peril of hide? Cross out my schoolbook's boastful claim: *securety of contiens* did not mean freedom of speech, but its opposite. To transplant a world, they had to interpret it. They did: *speech* was a form of *pestilence*. So witness this: one initial terrific and lengthy blast against profane swearers, blasphemers, Sabbath breakers, and *others of the ungodly*, to be fined, whipt, or utterly ruined. Added, it seems, as camouflage for the same penalties promised to any *pson or psons . . . inhabiting residing traffiqueing trading or comerceing within this Province or Within the Ports Harbors Creeks or Havens* who dared to speak ill of one another, as Heriticks, Scismaticks, Idolators, Puritans, Independants, Prespiterians, Popish priests, Jesuites, Jesuited papists, Lutherans, Calvenists, Anabaptists, Brownists, Antinomians, Barrowists, Roundheads, Sepatists. *Who shall at any time utter or speake any such reproachfull Words.* Acknowledg the Scandall and offence. Bee publickly whipt. Bee careful.

For it would not work, not yet, this clever compromise between *privacy of conscience* and its enemies. William Claiborne and his fellow avengers waited in the wings, while the Sussquehannocks captured the Piscatoway *King of Pawtomeck*, sacked storehouses along the Patuxent, killed Englishmen eight miles from St. Mary's City. The capital now had fewer men than had sailed in the *Ark* and *Dove*.

cold stream in a colder country
brow, breast, elbow, knee
indelicacy in the mingling

now sit every man in the readiest place

incantation ,striking blows
this metir graithed
for ravens

No court of appeal for the losers, Patuxents and Piscataways, who had suffered long for their Calvert friends; and not much gain for the victors. Claiborne signed a treaty with his old friends the Sussquehanough, who thus gained a safe southern border and freedom to make war on the Iroquois. War that would keep the English safe from the north for a generation. And spell the end of the Sussquehannocks, of the beaver trade, of their great, fortified capital on the river named for them. Thirteen acres palisaded. Three thousand survivors, out of six. Of the *purple rash*, scarlet fever, of measles mumps malaria, smallpox whooping cough and syphilis. For a decade they captured enemies in order to adopt them, while their own *disappeared* resurrected as Iroquois.

I afterward queried my companion
there being land enough and more

brattle : clatter
bray : enmesh

eagle and osprey   little roe deer
long gaze   of the vanishment

Old-Fields

And wherein shall we find their countrie? In 1652, three hundred and thirty crude plantations strung up and down the Patuxent. Fifteen hundred immigrants—masters and servants, women and children—stealing each other's indentured labor and buying corn from *the naturals*. Reselling same at a thousand pounds tobacco to the barrel. A small man's country: land and hand tools, cows in the woods. Lord Calvert's manorial fantasy dead in the wreckage of Ingle's thugs. *Original Lists of the Quality:* they worked their own fields and married late. Few children lived. Wee cottages of wattle and daub. Or post-frame houses with storage pits, less valuable than the nails that built them.

> *In Shirts and Drawers of* Scotch-cloth *Blue*
> *With neither Stockings, Hat nor Shooe*
> *These* Sot-weed *Planters Crowd the Shoar*
> *In Hue as tawny as a Moor*

For *that Stincking weed of America* in Maryland was a great Leveller. *Without the help of man, horse, or ox.* Just girdle the trees, plant hills of tobacco beneath the dying branches. No manure. No plough. Both cattle and pigs lived in the woods, with the wolves and the hunger and mire. Land was cheaper than labor, for men died so *prolifically*. Three good hands, who could work six acres, maybe seven, *according to the goodness of the ground,* needed twenty or thirty or more for the long haul. They learned to cut the leaves far back, to cure on the stalk instead of stringing, to find the right soils, to rotate with corn. Three years at tobacco, three years at corn, then fallow a generation. New land to be cleared each year. They farmed, that is, like Indians.

Would trade for their cultivated land
Indian Old-Fields   aggredation
whose natural womb by her plenty maintains
Degrees and Diversities
Colledge of Coyn
And each years Traffique to thy self get more
wherein are trees not cut, but girdled
sins not removed, but tolerated
Thus slovenly   and the admiration
dared not to adventure anything

Without old-fields it was three months clearing, a year till harvest and two till profit, how many hills of corn per acre, how many stumps, *illegitimate leaves*, tobacco barns *for the purity*. No soil here for the *Sweet,* so grow the *Oronoco.* Oyster shells in the middens as large as a man's hand. Two women or don't even think of a dairy: *necessariness of servitude.* Hoggs multiply, but cattle mire. Bring with you into this country a bushell of Pease, one gallon of Oyle, one suite of Cloth, six paire of shoes. Inkle for garters. Sugar, bay salt. One pot, one caske, one Frying-pan, with Platters, Dishes, and spoones of wood. In apparell, in bedding, in Armes, in tooles. Six pounds in passage. Trade out your swine. *Remember if any servant dies, the goods of that servant being sold will returne all his charge with advantage.* Some years more died than lived. Soap and candles. Iron wedges. Handsaws and Shovells, Nailes of all sorts. Grindstone, whip-saw, two hammers, five Howes. A Water-Spaniell could not do ille. Or nothing at all. The clothes on your back. Shipped by grace of God in good order.

whereof one man's part will bee

pipestone in the shape of animals
path internalized
whose   capture

offer it with two hands and reserve the ashes

So they built their towns on Indian towns. Well-situated, *cleared to my hand*. As trails disappeared in wickits of fire. And something dangerous evolved in the calming heart of tobacco. That sacrament. That spirit bridge. A *copulative matrimony* of typhoid and malnutrition. Average age at death: 48. In Massachusetts, at the same time: over 70. *To be extirpit and ruitit out*. Plant with the unseen power of a storm.

five-eighths among the immigrants
nine-tenths of the *country people*, loving and kind

Among the corpses, which was the genocide?

•

Each hour speaks in silent acts
of our Adamitical state

Refractory
and brute amaze
Palisade
against the Virgin

•

Yet once they were gone we had great difficulty
warlike habits and trails immaculate
forest so like a beaste and now

probable that we must not be explicit
Spaniards counted excessively and along the coast impossible

estimates listed in tabular form
fishing weirs we cannot emulate
by region, by tribe

prove the condition of savagery

(if dogs could be but trained to hunt
the Indian as they now hunt bear...

that the beaste might die   twice

*

Pagan *n* [ME fr late L *paganus*, civilian (*i.e.* not a soldier of Christ) fr L *paganus*, country dweller, from *pagus*, village, country] (14thc) **1**: a person who is not a Christian, Moslem, or Jew; heathen **2**: one who delights in sensual pleasures, material goods [IE *pag*, to fasten more at *pact* **5a**: L *pagus*, boundary staked out on the ground **b**: pagina, trellis to which a row of vines is fixed, hence (by metaphor) column of writing, page]

silence in feather
ransack   as the body withers

allocate   traverse
savage from the root of *sylvan*

Along the Potomac: Pascatoways; along the Patuxent: Patuxents, Aquintanacks, Yoacamocos, Assamacamocos, Matapannayens—farmed outside their new palisades, planting corn among the dead forms of girdled trees. Able-bodied and want not wit. *Little birds of the bignesse of sparrows.* 1652: a Scotsman. Arrived in the Royal colony of Maryland.

Heath

n [ME *hèthe*, fr OE *haeth*, akin to Ger *heide*,
wasteland, fr IE base *kaito-*, forested or
uncultivated land] (before 12c) **1:** a tract
of open wasteland, esp. in the British Isles;
moor **2:** any plant of the heath family (esp.
of genera Erica and Calluna); heather—
one's native heath the place of one's birth
or childhood

Alexander *sumtyme MacGregor,* of Clan Skilled, Clan Landless, robbed of Elec-
tion, possessed of employment, arrived a prisoner of war. After five years at hard
labor, bondsmen might receive freedom and *headright* to fifty acres—prisoners
and immigrants, alike, indentured to the promise. New men were sold, then left
to season a few months in the lethal climate. And if he survived. Each man *come
out of his time* had first to *find* his fifty acres, pay the surveyor and the clerk. Fifty
acres, without labor—worth less than a good cow. Three men to turn ten acres
to use, with one expected to die before the harvest. Debts payable in days of
work, collectible from a dead man. To *own labor*—that was wealth. Importers of
men earned their own headrights, or a thousand pounds (tobacco) on each man
or woman. A seasoned hand brought twice as much, for he was less likely to die.
Only one jail in the colony. For criminals, debtors, rescued defectors—brought
back from refuge with the Indians—: punishment was not confinement but bond-
age: indenture could be extended into smoke.

> *He spake of the temple of his body*
> trafficke in human boundary
> reddendum

47

The largest harbor in the world, great navigable rivers, a whole continent be-hind—*nothing done in anie one of them, but all is vanished into smoke*. Laws re-quired an acre of corn for so many acres tobacco. But who was counting? Servants who petitioned the court—too little food and too much work—sentenced to thir-ty lashes for their crime. Trafique is Earth's great Atlas, and *leaf* was, by then, the currant Coyn. Great protection against robbery. *Nor to dirty their Fingers by telling of vast sums*. Twenty-five percent of British customs. Five percent of the Treasury. A seed smaller than mustard seed. Those who owned landing places, by which it reached ship and sea, owned everyone.

power at the level of a molecule
chain unseen storm to the currency
a fair trafficke   in sacred

Alexander arrived well-armed. And may God bless the goose's quill, honored and ancient resident in the temple of property. Unlikely he ever touched a hoe. His indenture was perhaps one year, *servitor* to two illiterate men, whose land grants to him were signed with the mark of X. Skilled men could bargain—carpenters, brewers, bee-keepers—or sell their services on the side, purchase their freedom in a year or so. There must have been family money. There must have been pull. It is possible [read: *we take up this story where the rats left off*] he ransomed himself—with the gold chain Scots mercenaries wore in case of capture.

literate five hundred years
palisade only as good
as its description

2

Alexander MacCrouther / McGrowder / MacGrugir / McGruder / Magruder was the son of Alexander, the same, second husband of Margaret Campbell Drummond, of Keithick and Balmaclone. She was Drummond by her first marriage, Campbell by birth and by Act of Legitimation: her grandfather a Cistercian Abbot of Coupar Angus, priest-abbot until the Reformation, a member of the Convention of Estates, who on 17 August 1560 annulled the Pope's authority in Scotland. Grandmother unpreserved as the moorhen's footstep.

ink very black   *one can hardly resist*
this reference to representation

to search for other parts of their bodies
nearly concealed or passing into

that I beheld, and I a creature
(figure concealed by restlessness)

So: Margaret Campbell. She married, first, Andrew Drummond, cousin to the third Lord Drummond. His death left her in lifetime possession of Balmaclone, now Belliclone, a manor house and farm in the charter lands of Inchaffray: a widow of some property, during cycles of famine and sword. Abduction of her person meant possession of her land.

rape   as   ambition

Better to yield to necessity, *thing in this world that I best luf,* and marry. She chose, second, Alexander McGruder, Chamberlain to James Drummond, Lord Commendator of Inchaffray Abbey—his procurator. Of land. *In the ceremony of giving sasine, possession was transferred before witness of something symbolic, such as earth and stone.*

Aye, he married it

Margaret was thirty-four years old. She held Balmaclone—née Balmakgillon, Hamlet of the Sons of the Servant of John. One wall she touched still stands. I was there: east of Comrie on the old Perth Road. All interest in the farm belonged to her Drummond children. Thus Alexander the Younger, her eighth surviving child, would make no future there. He was seven when his father died and again his mother married—a Campbell cousin, and an officer, mercenary in obscure Continental wars. Alexander then, according to custom, sent to his father's people at Craigneich, Rock of the Raven. Or so we assume, since we don't know better. Since all we know is the name—Craigneich, Craigneish, *Craignight Plantation*—laid down on 200 acres of half-cleared Maryland woods.

peril of my gratitude
this black umbilicus   affection
bloody silence carried in you
or into

some would go hunting   I would go

in rock sanctum   hawk or hound
a bairn's part of gear   thy fastness

Ah, but never trust a *fair copy*, words by which the violence of revision is concealed. Go back along the drove roads, test the difference: mountains, or a view of the mountains. Like his father, Alexander was a younger son, and like his father landless—though *warranted*, you might say, by the left wing of a goose. His grandfather, James, the first MacGrowther named in ink as *servand to the Lord Drummond*—was witness, perhaps accomplice, to the *legendary anger of the Drummonds*, who, in the fervor of Reformation, *pat furth one great pairt of the native tennentis and puir laboris into utter hership and beggerte*. They were not put out, these McGrouthers. New walls rise on belovèd ruins: they were a privileged caste, and they adapted.

No kingdome lackes her own disease
a fine, tall theory
bronze plaque bolted tae the stane
or lack of it

Now penmanship my only fortune
legible hand, unfaded ink

of black wool and fine heather
red hand and the reddened edge

Puir pepelis, the inhabitaris
ground to walk   the open air

what happens to them   *anything
worth carrying is gone*

3

Alexander was twenty-eight years old when most of Scotland's noblemen signed the Covenant, and Presbyteries began to dispose of dissenters. Lesser folk subscribed—they could hardly avoid it—*publickly, with uplifted hand*—and paid a new tax on rents to fund the Covenant's army. Each landowner to appoint two men to *tak noteis off quhat armes they haue presenttllie, to wit, quhat muskittis,* and then to cause all able men be presentt at Perth vith thameselffis, 26 July 1638, at ten of the clock. An army at first independent, but within five years allied with the English Puritans—*Ane uthir sort, more miserabill*—whom they had vowed to convert to their own Scottish Kirk. (Item: an onion is always helpful *to annoynt the place that is bittin vith ane madde dog.*)

what thrift absolve an elegance
wind-tight, towering, God-driven sails

the heron stands on one leg in a dead tree on the bay

come fierce report   an agony
that I a man   and lakkith libertee

Of the Drummond Lords—those King's Ambassadors, Lords of the Bedchamber, *natural cavaliers* yet, for all their Protestant sturt and strife—we know that some raised regiments out of their tenantry, fought in the first and easiest sallies of the Covenanting army. That one was a *waiter on providence*, uncommitted till it seemed the tale was told. That two, including the Earl of Perth, signed the Covenant *and* Montrose's secret Band of Cumbernauld—to uphold the king and the Lord's *true* Covenant against all opposition. That one was *a loose and profane man*, with a sense of honor biographers find lacking in the rest. That all were related, many times over, to the *ruthless royalist* Montrose. That one changed sides on the way to battle, September 1644. That one received, in the following August, payment for forty bolls of meal supplied to the army Montrose was fighting. Or, rather, that James McGruther, Alexander's brother—Chamberlain to the Earl of Perth—received on his behalf.

scholars who can read this script
—merchantable commoditie—
becoming slightly drunk as the poem progresses
(o reddish bracken, golden broom)
that path   to a killing

What can we say of this James Makruther, to luif him weill and do him na skaith? Of his mind we know nothing, of his heart: less. But *in grammar something leads and something follows,* so let us look back a hundred years, to find his grandfather *put to the horn* for coming with David, the second Lord Drummond, to beseige Queen Mary's governor, at Leith. And then look forward: to March, 1649, a bare month after the king's beheading. *Leist God theirof tak haistie vengeance*: new regiments raised to make war on England, defensive plans against Cromwell's invasion, and James m^cgruder, styled Laird of Cargill, sits on a committee of war.

's rìoghail mo dhream
lion's head
erased in metrical vow

from Banqueting House to the scaffold
forged dishonest instigator

change thy mirth to melancholy
ah!

And Alexander? Of him we know precisely this: November, 1622: one Alexander McA Growder arrested for bearing arms, deer-hunting, shooting fowl—along with some Drummond and MacGregor lads. He was twelve; they were near Cargill. The rest is largely feather-dust: *tradition has it; is believed to . . .* Well, never mind. Official records concerned themselves with land-owners and eldest sons. And there was war. And paper burns so quickly once the ink has dried.

window now without its glass
clear view of what we came for

a calligraphic pedestal   in trees

scholars at the altar cloth
consult in order to disregard

footpath can't be followed on the sea

For twenty-four years from that teen-age arrest, Alexander appears nowhere in the kingdom of ink. He does not marry. He does not die. He does not give or receive in the name of his lord. He does not witness. He is not arrested. He is not cautioned to keep the peace. Minor clerk to the Drummonds? Perhaps. Scholar at Dunblane? Perhaps. Name lost to English soldiers burning abbey records to keep warm through a long winter? Perhaps. Or did he, as a lad of eighteen, follow his stepfather down to some port, *put his foot on board a ship*, sell himself to the Continent's wars?

how track   a deer slayer
out of kingdom's reach

for once our sources uncontaminated
fixity of symbol and
an unnatural interest in   restraint

[check prisoner lists and ladings
study the operation of 17th c. [blank]
translate [blank]
ask archivist to check the date

[palisade in flames
no utterance]

remark that the family retains a suspicion of Catholics

walk the perimeter

overcome fear of men encountered in darkness

ENCOUNTERS IN DARKNESS:

Gillawnene MacCrouther, James, John. Witness charter of 1447 by Patrick de Cumre to John de Cumre, for lands in Cumry, Kapaleany, Glenmayok. Page to Lord Drummond. Scribe to Lord Drummond. Bands of caution, witness or named. Raid with Lord Ruthven and Protestant lords on Leith, 1547. Declared rebel for raid on Livingstones, 1580. Died at Craigneich, or was there. Born at Craigneich, or was there. Took John Makintalgart prisoner. Took 100 pounds Scots money, three milk cows, and household goods. Killed lawless Mac-Gregours, 1612. Charged with Malcolme MacGregor and others, 1622. Born at Craigneich, or was there. Died at Craigneich, or was there. Fined for deer-hunting at Spittalsfield, Capputh Parish. Records of the Privy Council, Registrum magni sigilli regum Sc. orum Jacket II.

lie in wait   return arrayed
in perilous

thou unsaid
my gratitude

extractive industry foresworn

—
56

4

And where then shall we find their countrie?
the very roots from which we grew
What to weave   how to shrink it
strong arm of the alphabet   made full

(or knots unraveled   perilous)

Writing commences rather small
at the top of 4b grows larger
writer appears to have inherited
hunter god   with knife, hawk, hare
Or is it *horse*?   no right is proved
the god of death shape-shifting to a deer

Words in the margin with a line around them
shows where they belong
1a blank, 1b two human figures
and who owe fidelitie?

First to raise smoke and boil water
Near a great rock on the west side, or

barter the chase and mountain joy
untracked heath of the narrative

Girec
Gilawnene
Grùdair or *Cruitir*
each alone the violence   of the book

For with Columba out of Ireland came: motif of angels holding books, a *pointed hand*, or cursive, *secular Irish restlessness* condensed to the tip of a feather. 6th century: a foot trail, and a grand plan to convert the Picts. By white martyrdom of solitude, green martyrdom of exile: make a dysart in a *thin* place, *where the fabric between God and the world is frayed*. 7th century: a coin toss: two Irish missionaries, casting lots at the head of the River Tay. Fillan got Glen Dochart and the easy life of Strathearn. Adomnán got Glen Lyon, long, sere, difficult, and *thin*.

onto the moment   onto the gaze
swept backward into pure rock
mist from the steep of the brae
avalanches

herd of red deer in profile against the trees

forum can mean a marketplace
a court, a medium, a door
black points of punctuation
in which negotiation and   repent

love swept to earth
it bends where it can

erratic edge   of dalliance

Both Picts and Gaels were Christian, though of different sects. Both Picts and Gaels spoke Celtic, in dialects unintelligible: every book that survives is penned in Irish. Pictish words reduce to riddles, their art to an idiom we do not speak: z-rod, mirror-and-comb, hounds interlaced like ribbons down the edge of a vellum page. One word means *city, monastery*: monastic villages ruled by abbots, centers of literacy and art, of agriculture and fine brewing—they turned from austere St. Peter to passionate St. John. For whom beauty was holiness.

> deliberate avoidance of real resemblance
> (inkpot secured to the arm of a chair)
>
> in ornamentalist dialect
> lion and stag, wildcat and leaf
> original sinew   un-phrased

Now gospel of presence in an artifact: only pencils allowed in the reading rooms. Or, purchase their penmanship: sweat distilled to pure design, well-produced books of absences. Their stock was praise—same coinage as the local lads, illiterate illuminators, who raised each painted letter like the glorious body of Christ. We track their desires in the margin: fern leaf clusters, reliquaries, a hurried, crude stroke of the pen. Doodles of dogs' heads, bird, hare, deer. *A holy figure with stag's antlers*: sometimes they wrote poems.

Alas o my great lord of the elements
bad Latin   Pict motif
with raised hands extended

in lamp black   and orpiment
ground glass with gold suspended

where all women are the mother of god

vellum thick and not well-cleaned
St. John worked into profusion

the adder lies in the corbie's nest
—usual mark of contraction—

two rats nibbling eucharistic bread
and hairst o' glory

But first there was Adomnán, in the long, crooked glen. To him are attributed monasteries, footprints in rock, miracles, and *the first law in heaven and earth for protection of noncombatants*. All this from *a mere laddie*, armed with Holy Orders, a saint's staff and a hand bell. What did he have to do to win this dark heather, hillocky sponge? Preach at the round caistealan on the hills. Preach at the standing stones, prayer stones. Cast out devils and disease. In combat with a goddess, one-eyed and shadow-faced, whose name he most carefully did not preserve.

cold stream in a colder country
one hawk, one hound   a demon lover
lazing in   or all of it

5

At the foot of Glen Lyon, now, the village of Dull. Scatter of houses, a church, a farm, three stone boundary crosses. Close by, the village of Fortingall: a 3000-year-old yew tree, two damaged rings of standing stones. *There was at Dull a great Monastery*—abthanerie, in the local parlance. *Abthanus:* Scots Latin: father of thanes. *Thane:* a minor nobleman. Or *abdhaine*: Gaelic: abbacy. It stood at a crossroads—an ecotone—where narrow footpaths and tilted granite spill into the flat and fertile straths. *Great*, in this case, meant a clutch of buildings, some no more than a roof with dry stane walls, housing a clutch of Culdees—Friends of God—that under-organized set of local scribblers and hermit saints, saying its mass in *some barbarous rite* and not obeying bishops . . . until the Crown converted, 12th century, to Rome. And to feudal hierarchies of surnames, primogeniture, and government by *breve*. With minted coin and heavy horse—which cost a hundred pounds apiece, and each knight needed three. A great religious overhaul, *for* which Queen Margaret was canonized, *by* which the old abthaneries passed into chartered estates. By the 14th century, Dull stood in the growing desmene of Sir John Drummond—a *thane* no more, but *barron* of Cargill, ambitious and ready for more.

extracted tongue of the sacrament
o signature   absolve

Nay, to go forward
with the confidence and resolution of a Man

Gilawnene McCrouder—*that is, and no error,* Gille Eonain, *servant of Adomnán, as Bede writes it.* Witness to a charter of land, he signed at Comrie on March 10, 1447. *Combruidh*—confluence—at the mouth of Glen Artney, twenty miles from Dull, where Lednock and Ruchill Waters pour into the Earn. *Strathearn*: a broad river valley at the Highland Line. Earthquake country, in its own small way, *right noble expanse* of Roman camps; of old black forest and standing stones; of marsh and bogland ditched into service; rich farms, castles, raw steep hills; and sky.

what is a mountain?
many births
what can't be forged   intransitive

change their sound in the midst of words

traditionary poetry   footprint
anent your grave

As witness, and literate, Gilawnene MacCrouder was *surely a Culdee of Dull,* and from him we acquire a name, a grammar of descent through sons, where *mac,* son of, becomes a kind of property—heritable, transferable, and harder to destroy than silver coin. MacGrùdair, son of the brewer? Or daughter—NicGrùdair, as it would have been, daughter of the brewer. Or perhaps NicCrowther, daughter of the musician? *Crowd* or *cruit,* a stringed instrument, now obsolete. Or take it in Irish, MacCruitir, son of the harper? A name *reasonably scarce* and spare—perhaps as old as one Gilcolinus Makgugir, named as witness in a case at law, on 12 February, 1264, at Dull.

           moss   sedge   bracken   broom
                archival trove   or obstacle
           extant correspondences   cold
                     as I expected

           thirty-one miles of metal shelves
           water where you step or kneel

                     hill path   in

After Gille Eonain, a scatter of names through Glen Artney, then east to Craig-
neich and Drummond-earnoch, to Crieff, Innerpeffray, Madderty, Perth—a map
for the most part matching the spread of the Drummond family through Strat-
hearn. *Conques or keip thingis conquest to thy hand*: the motto of their kind—
whose walls were stone, whose weapons steel. Any literate man was a useful man,
a pretty feather in their nest—or was it pinion in their arrow?—as they gathered
up lands and charters, farms and rents, by all the usual methods: foreclosure of
debt, protection of widows, marriage, royal favor, murder.

                stand at a window set in a wall
                that now connects to nothing

                workmanship creates a view
                     castle   or a naked hill
                lit stone   or an undressed body

           fashioned and reduced unto a method

Duncan McGrode, 1455. Christian McAcruter, 1463. Donaldo McGruer, Kathrine NcCrewar. McGrugor, McRewir, McRury, McRewyr, McCreuar. *Very few and lame are the documents* but certain the topography: testators, witnesses, plaintiffs, tenants: in a landscape of barley, oats, and cattle; of stockmen, hay-cutters, linen-weavers; earth floors, in houses shared with stock, whose bodies warmed the winters—they were born and died, married and cautioned, disputed boundaries and claimed their debts, entirely at the pleasure of the Drummond Lords. A prosperous family had a good roof; the rest got by. Privies, chimneys, window glass, soap—all unknown. It was said a Highland man, woman, or child could run up-hill and vanish in the time it took a nobleman's factor to dismount from his horse. Though *it is said* means little more than mud.

<blockquote>

now red wheat waves on smoother plains
each ear of corn carries its full burden

uncut pages   water stained
wherein temptation   certainty

if slash, foray, smoothly woo
to puzzlement   unformed consent

mercy it is   that winter fact
affectionate fame   of the conqueror

</blockquote>

6

1488, and history begins when it changes: in the person of young James IV, whose henchmen murdered his father to make him king. At sixteen, putty in his elders' hands: he would perform penance all his life for that betrayal. Yet he was, despite all, a Renaissance king, *interested in everything*. In ships, in guns, in tournaments; in clothes, music, and surgery; in alchemy, language, government—he even learnt a little Gaelic—in the sick, the poor and *restless riding*—plagued by *wyld wikkid Hielandmen* all his life. His only faults a lengthy beard and a tendency to wander. Father, in song, to a family of *beggarman* ballads—in which some poor but kindly maiden is first seduced, then carried off to be queen, by a bright-eyed stranger in rags. Father, in fact, to a small collection of royal bastards by a large collection of mistresses—high-born women to whom he gave lands, power, and husbands; and *bair ars* women to whom he gave money and a rare good time.

hussies or *housies*   mind your spelling
on goat vellum   not well cleaned

ane stone the size of a hen's eg
or ground glass in the offering

The hand round which I lived so long
bound now to blows   intransigence

Between my legs   one horse
one hawk   one hound

So here's a good yarn, spun round one of the king's women—Margaret Drum-mond, eldest daughter of the first Lord Drummond: that so long as she lived the king would not marry, or *could* not, having been secretly married to *her*. That she and her sisters were poisoned—perhaps by rivals, perhaps by their father's own hand—to make way for another Margaret: a royal alliance with Margaret Tudor, sister of Henry VIII. Like most such legends it was born well after the fact. Though it's true she was housed at the king's castles. And true she bore him a child—a daughter, by providence, raised at court. And true that this daugh-ter's official companions included two African women, one of whom presided as Queen of Beauty at the king's most lavish tournament, staged in June 1507, shortly after the birth of his first legitimate child.

> *Lang heff I maed of ladyes quhytt*
> *Nou of an blak I will indytt*
> her short cat nose
> her mekle lips

> whose cause the *nycht* would gladly fight

> Poet in a rhyming, punning frolic
> tar-barrel no quarrel with rich apparel
> *rode to the joust in chair triumphal*
> and lips ships eclipse

Oh, fun while it lasted, whatever it meant—the jousting, like everything else in life, laden with symbols we can't now read. Lord Drummond—raised to that title by the old king, James III—had changed sides neatly, close counselor now to the upstart son. A skilled ambassador, was it he who arranged the marriage of his king to Margaret Tudor?

Alliances, promises, loyalties—who needs them? 1513: this popular king, this randy king, *who to poets never made refusal*, made good on his promise to France. Invaded England to draw off forces from the French war. And thus died fighting his brother-in-law's army, at Flodden, taking 10,000 Scots and most of the aristocracy with him.

> idiot hand elected flesh
> probable to the difficulty

> rowan berry   drop of blood
> upturned phallic bud at the branch end

To Scotland he left an infant monarch, James V, just one year old. Imprisoned by his Regents, at sixteen this James escaped to France, then did his father one better: died when his wee daughter, Mary, was a mere *week* old.

> by incantation   striking blows
> the precious seed entrusted
> (someone had to clean up after
> throw dry soil over the blood, and sweep)

But nothing in that brutal century seemed to unseat the Drummonds. While Henry VIII celebrated his victory; while clergy rehearsed their new Catechism, in Scots, lest they *stammer and stumble;* while John Knox rowed in a prisoners' galley, and the Beggars' Summons called rich friars out to serve the poor; while France and England fought over Scotland's *Little Queen,* and printers became a suspect race, for printing *ballattis, sangis, blasphematiounis, and rhymes*, the Drummonds navigated all—like a kayak built for frothy waters.

fragments of illumination
at cattle market   stolen ground
by other names   recklessness

Note of all Warrants for the Granting of Land
indelicacy   in their mingling

Early deaths—with one execution for murder—cleared out most of the first Lord Drummond's heirs, but he lived long enough to see his great-grandson, David, inherit—who, with other Protestant Lords, assembled at Perth to assault the Catholics fortified at Leith. Who saw France driven off Scottish soil, and Parliament (in one week's work) take leave of the Pope and exile the Mass (but allow poetry to sneak back in, through the *Psalms*). Lord Drummond and his retinue—with all of those rebellious lords, their pages, their sons, and their chamberlains—were granted remission in the uneasy truce that began Queen Mary's reign. Some even say his two boys, Patrick and James, were educated with James VI, Queen Mary's son.

Not good to be of ill-famed race
Not good to neglect the dogs
And not good to o'er praise   necessity

Can read and write, will pass as free
Has a very plausible tongue

Or so they say—

If you go to the trouble of erasing
holes in the paper   gradual sprawl
of every kind of render

Schoolmates or not, the Drummond boys made out well under James VI, who showered them with titles. To James Drummond, the younger brother: Lord Commendator of Inchaffray Abbey, Gentleman of the Bedchamber, and 1st Lord Madderty. While the biggest plum went to Lord Madderty's nephew, the 4th Lord Drummond: created 1st Earl of Perth in 1605, two years after James VI was reborn as James I.

Pity the men whom you may spoyle
in density of usefulness

though force and freedom may be foliage
cleare contrarie to the common use

in dei nomine amen   counted
as a pen test

So who took care of business, while these Lords were at play in the fields of power? Factors, chamberlains, procurators. Not *ordinary tenants*, they would later claim, but *special friends* of their Drummond sponsors, and canny enough in their own upward scramble. James MacGrowther, in Craigneich, Page to the 2nd Lord Drummond. *Granted remission for rebellion,* along with his master and the other lords who besieged Queen Mary's governor at Leith. He married a Drummond, and two of his sons thus rose above him: John—who through marriage obtained a charter of land in Glenartney—was Chamberlain to the 3rd Lord Drummond. And Alexander—our Immigrant's father—Chamberlain to Lord Madderty. *Witnessed, in 1603, the testament of his predecessor, Thomas Drummond of Drummond-earnoch.* Dead by 1617, Alexander did not see his sons grow up—his younger son sold to America; but his older son, James, a canny survivor in the Reformation's deadly sport: a land-owning laird at Cargill, and Chamberlain to an earl.

incurvature   incondite
or emulate   (illegible)

sheaves of paper, all of it inked
broomrape   reddedum   recite

that signature of a solitude
—I meant to say *an servitor*—

right of sword-word-sword

anent

In the Stranger's Land

Stray through the woods but carry nothing
possible body isled in me
(revise)
to harp player   man with a cup
figure concealed by intricate path
strife   in hands of a binder

Now yawning over the manuscript
—chemical stained in the last century—
taste its fruit when it was red
I have made only trifling changes

Drop a crumb, spit in the fire
children hereafter to be born
in stasis   of perplexity

1649—that chaotic year, when Charles I met the heading axe. Lord Calvert: struggling to keep his colony. Alexander MacGruther: a traveler not found on any map. Nor any deed. Nor any regiment. At Preston, 1648, Dunbar, 1650: Scots prisoners in large numbers. 1651, Lord Madderty's brother commanding a regiment at Worcester, captured along with most of his men. And *not to be idle burdens to their captors*: one hundred fifty Scots prisoners transported. One ship, the *John*, lost at sea; and one, the *Guinea*, docked at St. Mary's City, 1652. 1653: *Alexander Macruder* takes oath to receive. Land. In the Royal Colony.

Among all our joys   ˙there is no one

In the 1650's, survivors among the Mattapanients, Aquintanacks, and Patuxents signed a treaty and moved together to a Mattapanient townsite up-river from the English. [So much say now the histories. In the lexicon of the ethno-historian: *Scotsman* spelled *Englishman*.] The settlers soon leap-frogged that sanctuary: Alexander's eighth plantation, Good Luck, lay upstream from the reservation. He already owned an Assamocomaco cornfield, a strip of priceless alluvial soil he called Magruder's Landing. He already owned Inchaffray/Anchovray/Anchovie Hills, the height above. He had taken the oath. And signed his name. In twenty-one variant spellings.

100 acres Magruder's Beginning
500 acres Good Luck
200 acres Alexander's Hope
250 Dunblane
500 Magruder Landing
200 misspelled Craignight
400 acres Anchovie Hills
in the Freshes of Aquasco Creek

Surveyed for him from a point of speech: *marvellously wasted*
From thence through the woods as far

A great part of the people of Accomacke
Not the sixth Savage in two hundred miles
Not then as many hundreds as they had been thousands
In no place but where we had been

In some townes about twentie, in some fortie, in one sixe score
That they neither knew what it was nor how to cure it

Stratigraphy
Metaphysicks
Ten thousand years of inhabitation
An indenture in which the one hundred and fifty
Half so which were   widow

700 acres, the Indian Reserve, low-lying land at the mouth of the Western Branch.
Good wintering ground for geese. Plenty of malaria. Not one description of their
life there. What kind of houses, how many fields. Oyster shells on the middens
now no larger than thumbs.

Breathe for the simple
leap so whispered

to wander in the America
and untraveled parts of Truth

sometimes wake at night to the sound of bees
crouched in the full catastrophe
plenitude   as the measure of force

I arrived with a warrant
I execute
churring   itinerant   remorse

1654: Quiet in England, Cromwell installed. In Scotland, debt and starvation. In Maryland, the first hysteria of peace: Puritan repeal of the Act Concerning Religion: an open season. On Catholics, Jews, Quakers, and all dissenters. March 25, 1655: Battle of the Severn, an *unprecedented malignity* as pro-Calvert Protestant Governor Stone fought old Calvert enemy William Claiborne, on a Sunday. October 3, 1655: *Alexander Magrudder claimes of the estate of John Crabtree 170 pounds Tobacco.* 1660: the Restoration, of Charles II and a new Lord Calvert, of order and the Toleration Act. Beginning of the end of the beginning. 1661: Alexander Magruder *becomes possessed* of a landing.

> sweet the blackbird sings his song
> sweet the eagle over him

> sword in hand, head in the sand
> something to eat at nightfall

His second son was born that year. Second we know of. Not counting children in Scotland, gotten on a loved wife. Or soldier's whore. Or servant, farm-girl, tinker, daughter of some wealthy man he dared not face. Fifty-one years old, and a reckoning cut by water. So let us look back dispassionately. Let us look back statistically, erect new trees as he fells them: of freedmen who survived, three out of four got land. Of freedmen who survived, three out of four had a chance to govern themselves: as juror, constable, sergeant, councilor, JP, sheriff, militia officer. The price of tobacco was down but shipping was up. (He owned a *landing*.) The river there half a mile wide, with draft for ocean-going ships. Backed by Indian old-fields, flooded each spring so the soil did not die. His sons did not die. In a country of young immigrants, he was an old man. Had he been twenty-two, he could have expected to die at forty-four. He was fifty-one. *Fredome all solace.* The axe in his hands. Money and land and no debt, as fast as he could, for his sons.

black knife between systole   dyastole
the forme of binding a servant

sensation of sinking and rising
flight of pelicans low over brown water

in the stranger's land are plenty of wealth and wailing

Each man to produce one thousand pounds (tobacco) in a year, five to six thousand plants, and learn. To pack in hogsheads, not in bales. Freight charged by number, not by weight, so pack it well. Access to the landing charged in kind. Taxables tripled in twenty years, and every one of them had to ship. *Hold a pinch of tobacco above eye level. Offer it to the four winds.* More ground cleared but most woods wet: don't live there. Look for high ground, such as it is, and still call yourself a Highlander.

build a hill, knee high, two minutes

Houselot ½ acre: garden, and milking pen, 1 acre for orchard, 6 for corn. Law required 2 acres of corn to be cultivated per man that worked tobacco. Yield: 3–4 barrels shelled corn per acre. Legal ration: three barrels per man, including seed for next year. Store food and later garbage in the pits dug under your floor. Let rotting heat the long damp nights. One decade of your life what now they call *farm-building*. Watch it kill your neighbors, your servants, your wife. Get up each day to prepare the hills, transplant seedlings. Dream nights of smoke, of worming, topping, succering, cutting, pearing, hanging, stripping, curing, bundling, and prizing—into hogsheads—rolled to the landing.

don't bruise the fragile leaf

By the 1660s, up to fifteen-hundred pounds per acre and man. Or stoop down here and examine the dirt. Ceramics, scissors, straight brass pins, butter mold. There were women here. There was life, not measured in pounds. An iron padlock: something of value. *Wooden earthfast:* house to survive no longer than a man. Throw garbage out the window. Root pit near the fire. Welch chimney: mud and wood. Time plotted by the change in pipes: the clay, the shape, a maker's name. And scraps of flint, from strike-a-lights, gunflints. Wine-bottle glass, hearth ash, a coin, the DNA of human shit. Cow hooves, fish scales, crab claws, fruit pits, the bones of rabbit, deer, pig, grouse, duck, chicken, turtle, raccoon, squirrel, and dove. A finger ring, *Love the Giver,* brass buckle, thimble fragment, kettle fragment, bit and spur. Ceramics, some with brown salt glaze, some Indian and some imported, marked with the initials of the King.

> *but when I woke out of my dream*
> echo mocks the corncrake

> discontent and carry yourself
> *I found my bosom empty*

Anchovie Hills gone back to forest, rumor of a graveyard. Boat-launch at the landing, new houses on Dunblane: a strip mall and a theater. Marlboros for sale at the Quick Stop on Mattapanient Parkway. Goose preserve on the old Reserve at the mouth of the Western Branch.

beggarly and incident
signifies a frantique spirit

Waste intervening to the nearest enemy
she's bound his wound with a golden rod

element ground   of passing

•

Came he landless   subtle savage
Killed and reborn by the Ancyent Men

•

landing places for goods

unmanned wild country

codicil made in extremis

November, Magruder's Landing—now a public boat ramp on Magruder's Ferry Road. It's cold and damp. There's little to look at and nothing to do. From the Maryland Park Service tobacco barn—preserved and fitted out for edification—I steal a single leaf: brown, brittle, and half as long as my arm. In the treetops, some crows, noisy, and something white flashing among them. A gull? No, one of the crows has a white wing—entirely white. A pick-up truck pulls in, turns around, pulls out. I have neither camera nor dry socks (*presence of self on the long path*). In my notebook I scribble half-heartedly: date—time—place, the height of the cattails, the crow. The river is shallow, silted-in, a dull brown under the gray sky.

Wrath and steadfast in the one center

my mother lies dying of smoke

n [O.Sc. *hervist, hayrst*] (14c) **1**: harvest **2**:
autumn **3**: (19c) a harvest job, *esp* **tak a**
hairst engage oneself as a harvest labour-
er; (20c) **hae a day in hairst wi someone**
owe someone a favor, have a score to settle

1677:
Alexander dead
Came Samuel Taylor and Ninian Beall
overseers named in the Last Will and etc.
requesting to have the same proved
by oathes of witneses thereunto
that widow of the deceased
who is therin named executrix
with the orphans of the etc.
was lately dead
to have administration to them committed
of all and singular the goods
chattels and debts
two others appraisers and the said Jowles
[price of liquor set by the county]
Ninian Beall, Lieutenant of Militia
who served as representative
in dealings with the Indians
[we must not pass judgment upon a Law
according to one line

nor upon the large, extending bowels of America]
had once in his house four score of venisons
[plain bread rather was courted than desired]
and for long service with Indians
rewarded in old age...

but I digress
Elizabeth
said widdow and executrix
came in good health three months along
and shewed that shee the said Elizabeth
[estimates listed in tabular form]
being of sounde and disposing mind
that Ninian Beall
that Samuel Taylor
[let us flay and dress their several hides]
with letters testamentary
of said orphans, choir master
full survey of goods and chattels
[will annexed to the glossary]
Elizabeth, the last wife
retoured his heir
again

[heroick vigor that dwells in some kinds of beaste
I don't know why don't ask me]

O miserable tongue, don't lie. Land for tobacco, for corn, for fallow. Fifty acres per hand, to make it pay. Land for investment, land for landing. *Believe assuredly & inherit.* Timber and grazing and deer and geese. Three men to turn ten acres, the lethal climate. *Prepared for the Elect Chosen.* Land on both sides of the river. Warehouses. Docks. Two families, six children, to provide for: *that noe Contest may arise*: codicil, *made in extremis,* specifying the rights of the older three children, the younger three, survivors. Who to live where till the land is clear. What age to enter into. Land without labor: worth less than a good cow. *Witness my hand and seale this day, and first being sorrie for my sins.* Uneven blackness of bad ink, unmended pen: this *Kingdom prepared* on coarse parchment, texture of a homespun cloth. *The figure of a small man apparently in the act of jumping.* The figure of a small man, *misplaced as some maintain.* The figure of a small man, *the very place where he was hurried.* Rough-page-much-folded-red-wax-seal. Archival odor of great care. The figure of a small man, grown into a large one.

> 2 feather beds 4 blankets 2 pil-
> lows all old 2 pr candlesticks
> 1 table 1 cupboard 2 warming
> pans clothes cupboard coat-
> hang 2 joynt stools wood chairs
>
> 3 gunns 1 gridiron 6 old spoons
> 1 pr fire irons w/ 1 small pr [il-
> legible] 12 yards lining 4 of silks
> 2 browne thread 13 yards mixt
> searge long looking glass 1 desk
> 1 sealskin trunk all old

canoo with lock and chain 150 lb
1 man negro named Sambo 5000
lb John Land 4 years to serve
2000 lb Tho Jonas 6 years to
serve 2000 lb Elinor Murphy 7
years to serve 2000 lb Ann John-
son 1 year to serve 400

1 cart 1 cart saddle 4 iron pots
1 old 1 iron-bound case w/ 10
bottles 4 black-handed knives
nails 3 bibles small books old 1
copper pot tinn candlesticks ah
what does it matter debt on bill
debt by account

Maryland County Calvert Patux-
on The Inventory of the goods
and chattels of the late deceased

Alex: Magruder the 14 day
September 1677 a Totall Summ
48,776, with debt 1,148

5 bulls 10 heifers 16 cows 9
w/ calves 2 changes of coat &
britches (but many shoos) table
cloath & clothes of callago hose
of leather lambes 2 doz coarse
napkins no pipe

2000 lbs each, his servants. John Lande, a witness to his will: approximate value of a mare and colt. Sambo: from the price, a man in his prime. Most valuable property. Of *he that ay had livyt fre*. Or not.

> black man in a wool glengarry
> eye contact
> at the far edge of dalliance
>
> embarrassed merely to pronounce
> that Alexander's pen
> that mine
>
> a capture and
> it turns and shows its teeth

2

Something my mother told me: Ninian Beall, another Scotsman captured by Cromwell, exported like so much wheat to feed the appetite of the colonies. His sons and daughters married Magruders, became Magruders, his story now interlaced with theirs. Speaker of Indian languages, lieutenant of *a most thorough system of ranging*, authorized, by his Lordship's special command, to press a man and horse to speed intelligence. *For there were long the isolated murder expected of savage natures,* the occasional spree or tuilzie, the need to know the mood of the Indians during conflicts inglorious. Alexander's friend for his twenty-four years of inhabiting: Ninian Beall, with Samuel Taylor, went to the Testamentary Court and swore that Elizabeth, like her husband, was dead. Later a Burgess, later a boulder dragged into the Cathedral Close, to hold his name in the rain in perpetuity. A man of Signall Services, Laborious Endeavours, large land holdings. Rewarded in old age by the State Assembly, *for long converse with the Indians:* gift of three *serviceable* Negroes.

o ryvir   mee delyverit
a bataill broucht on bordour hard by us
has faire ourgilt oure speche

A serving wench   or conjurer
One man-negro   named

that in heil was   and gladness

straddled by this doolie dream

Something she never told me: fourteen slaves conspired to poison his grandson, John—husband of Alexander's granddaughter, Verlinda. Just one, *Beall's Bess,* convicted, sentenced to hang. In inventory of the goods and chattels: slave whip, lead bar in the handle. With great iron fetters for men's feet, small iron fetters for men's hands. *And by the extremity of the correction should chance to die.* Then not accompted felony, but a misjudged destruction of property. Or, try a tale like this: one slave (unnamed), killed by Indians (unnamed). The master (named) awarded sixty buckskins by the court. He had to collect from Piscataways. Who could not pay. He accepted land in the reservation for the life of an African man, fourteen yards of Broad Cloath and some beads. A simple three-way trafficke in *Remove.*

North and by West two hundred and forty perches
to a bounded oak of a parcel of Land

said alienacion shall be void
alike true to nature and history
in isle of caution   drifting face
fidelitie of the human beaste

No greater gift than a negro

Aye, and a gift in good time: indentured servants were so scarce even unmarried women worked out their term. Alexander had five sons, a daughter: all needed labor. Rolling depressions for forty years, price down and shipping sometimes not at all. Their only recourse was more tobacco, each man to produce more plants, more pounds, more *God knows what they thought of it*. Not one document records an attitude. For that egalitarian frontier of early death. For this new wedding, *weill wers than death*. This black solucioun, disputacioun, immortality of *human beast*.

Cattle and treasure the same word

in animal light of the tallow candles
a bedtime genealogy
ink smeared by a careful hand

Come tell me what they call ye

proud in his carriage, speaks little English
his wool is commonly combed back and tied
with remarkable good and White teeth
born in England and bred a farmer
born in Antigua, straight limbed
and when drunk stammers in his speech

Now yawning over the manuscript
yellow stain the color of a turtle's back

Whoever pursued what did not run
if measured by the pine trees

For those who could read, an underpinning (silk stitched to the osnabrig): a Neo-Platonic taxonomy of Angelicall, Rationall, Brutall. But this was the dawn of Enlightenment, so have the latest: Sir William Petty's *The Scale of Creatures*: mankind no longer a perfect whole, standing alone unassailable between Angel and Animal: an ambiguous place for the Savage, now, in the universal scheme. *Subsistence drawn from the forest,* or *well-tempered but disposed to Idleness.* Call it an ethnological breakthrough. In Maryland, 1664: *shall serve Durante vita*: call it *Law.*

> *I were climbing a tree that were too high for me*
> old-field pine on poorer soil   fierceness of a rainstorm

> tremulous calling   falling free

> All endit was my innocence
> *But throw me my irons, lad, for they cost me dear*

3

1634: Mathias de Sousa, an indentured mulatto, arrived in Maryland with the Jesuits he served. His name survives among the few, living under the same laws that governed Englishmen. The rhetoric of *human beaste*, perfected for the Irish, Highland Scots, and Indians, had not yet bothered with him. Free by 1641, he served for a time in the Maryland Assembly. 1644: no further record of de Sousa, and the first two slaves arrive in Maryland. Two years before, Leonard Calvert, the governor, had offered to trade all his land for seventeen slaves, but found no takers: in England, mercantile reform had not yet created the *slaver* as *businessman*.

> Copy the doleful words of another
> —bad print of a microfilm—
> where larks rose up, startled before me

> In fragments of illumination
> tools for breaking   keeping still
> what writer wadna gang as far
> as change-house keeper?

By the 1650s: *fragrance of their holy lives:* single slaves, or groups of two, of three or five, in hovels in the half-cleared woods. Most were past their working prime, or children, sold from Barbados or Virginia. Twenty or twenty-five pounds Sterling, each one of them, two or three times the headprice of indentured Englishmen. *Uneasiness under this exercise:* one in four died in their first year, *and fear to sleep in the bed of a dead man.* Speaking their various harshe dictions, un-named by their masters. *Hanged himself in ye old 40 ft Tob. house not any reason.* (For I had no person to speak to.)

Survival means   to answer
(one hand, two inks, a scorch mark)
overseer stands on a stump
Discover'd some behaviour in him

as lark discendis from the skyis hycht

most of the air dissolved in salt
provisions for another year
absent hammer   of laughter

Jack, Quacko   boy born on Wednesday
Jemmy, Quame   boy born on Saturday

Pheobe, Phibba   girl born on Friday
Phyllis, Fili   losing the way
to abandon   to deceive

In the stranger's land, an aptitude *proportionable to the tune*: how to eat, work, marry, shelter, raise a child. Slave ships carried two men for every woman: *preparation toward a Natural and experimental history*. Biafrans, Angolans, Nigerians. Ibos, Ibibios, Efkins, Mokos. Born in Africa, born in Barbados. Skilled in the art of tobacco; or not. Tracing descent from women; or not. In clans and lineages; or not. Had first to find, or make, a common language. Shocked into labor, underfed, *to make them more industrious.*

a Negro Quarter is a Number of Huts
And cultivate at vacant times, the little Spots allow'd them
(edge-stained, water-stained, upper margin illegible)

Not the hundredth Part of the Countrie clear'd, the High-Lands overgrown with Trees, the Low-Lands sunk to water. Ten months of work in every year, *as custome was* the drug trade. *As custome was:* standing water in footprints, shoe tracks, malaria, to which most Africans were immune. Pneumonia in the winter and spring, from which they dropped like flies. *As custome was*: distressed servants ran to refuge with the Indians. *As custome was* bewildered Africans ran to refuge with the Indians. Some to find freedom. Some to find wives. *As custome was* the Susquehannocks adopted them, the *Shewans*, the Piscataways. Adopted them and did not lie, when they told pursuing Rangers there was no one in their village but themselves.

Primitive and heroick work
to take an oath so wounding

Shall be Slaves for the terme of their lives

Burden of proof is on the plaintiff
disinherison, deprivation
interchangeably set their hands

Sundrie slaves   have of late Years run
some of which have perished and others encouraged
chin branded R   an ear cut off
You would really be Surpriz'd at the Perseverance

And took his hand, his soft hand

Something has strayed into this line from the next

4

1734: Nathaniel Magruder, Alexander's youngest son, deceased. At Inchaffray / Anchovray / Anchovie Hills: dwelling house 25 feet long, plank floor, one chimney, in poor repair. Negro quarters 10 feet long, in poor repair. Two 40-foot tobacco houses, in good repair. Milkhouse and garden with new palings, 262 apple trees, 1,494 panels of fence, 7 slaves. One, through age and lameness in her arms and hips, incapable of service, *and I pray no levie be laid for her.* An income of 1000 pounds (tobacco). A tenant farm bringing 600 more, with fruits of the orchard. In inventory of goods and chattels: horses called *Knight* and *Fox*, Negroes called *Prince* and *Lizard,* 2 old prayer books, 13 chairs, 52 pounds of pewter.

Better to be in the wood of wild rain
than vanish so   a country where

with gangs of cattle   disfrequent hogs
scattered shrubbery where a house had been

Honor admired in a looking-glass
What else can solace   what else gain

Crooked   but it leads away
from boundary

In the same year, Sarah Magruder died at Good Luck, a few miles away in the new county christened *Prince George's*. A niece or some-such of Ninian Beall? Some say yes, some say no, but without doubt widow of Samuel, oldest surviving son of Alexander's first American marriage. He bought and inherited farmland, town land, warehouse, store. Owned shares in a Pertuxson Merchant Ship. Paid tax, in 1682, of nearly 50,000 pounds tobacco. Dead by 1711, he left to his sons 1200 acres, investments, instructions, slaves. And to his daughters ten pounds each, *for to buy her a gown and a petticoat*. Sarah had land of her own to give: 300 acres called Head Ake, left to one daughter and one granddaughter. And silver tankards and silver spoons and Negroes—one each to nine named heirs in eight households. A canny division of root stock, of *brow, breast, elbow, knee*. Such hoeing and weeding, hairst and rain: by 1790, the first census, 45 Magruder households in three counties: 41 owned slaves.

tail of the beast terminates in leaf
small passion   pandemic waste
of effort planted to disguise

I lean'd my back unto an oak
I thought it was a trusty tree
But first it bow'd, and then it broke

that God in all his werkis   wittie be

I am reading a used copy of Edmund Morgan's *American Slavery, American Freedom* marked heavily in the first six pages. The handwriting is large and looping: female, unreflective, and young. On the first page she has underlined *slavery* and *slaves* twice each, *enslaved* once. In the margin: *obsessed by slavery.* After page six, she has underlined nothing until page ninety, where this fragment is heavily marked with brown felt-tip: *heathen savages was intolerable.* There is no other mark in the book until, on the end-papers, in pink highlighter, these large capital letters: *I HATE <u>HISTORY</u>!*

> engage an interpreter
> this   is a bibliography

5

1664, the Maryland Assembly—in between An Act for Ferrys and An Act for the Preservation of Harbours: that forasmuch as divers freeborne English women forgettfull of their free Condicõn and to the disgrace of our Nation doe intermarry with Negro Slaues. Etc. Such women to be exiled from the white territory of *lawful increase,* banished to the backlands of *natural increase.* The law took some tuning. In its first form, all such women, along with their children, joined their husbands in slavery for life. Later forms created a borderland, where for white and mulatta women alike the crime of *mulatto bastardy* brought seven years of servitude to the mother, thirty-one of indenture to the child. Which translates: all their most productive years, at hoe and forge and child-bed. All such unions defined as fornication, and all mulatto children illegitimate in advance. *Father* banished henceforth from the kingdom of ink. But *corporeal ingenuity* is difficult to trim. 1681: the first of three laws to stop unscrupulous masters and dames from breeding mulatto slaves on their white serving women.

at cattle market   stolen ground
such boundaries between words   within
this Sot-Weed or To'bo

For gif Nature be not the chief worker
(and twenty other curious points)

make welcome, m'lord   an history
that drynk be mynglet with mete

My serving girl Prissy, named in Sarah Magruder's will, valued at £15. Priscilla Gray was her full name, a mulatta described as *born of a white mother*. If her father was a free black man, Priscilla's indenture was twenty-one years; if a slave, thirty-one. Born around 1708, she might have been free by the 1730s, but with the birth of each of her children she was hauled into court and convicted, her term of bondage extended. Once, it was only for nine months, and the child sold for twenty-one years, so the father was a free man, maybe a white one; but in five other cases the child was bound for thirty-one years and Priscilla saw seven more years tacked onto her own sentence. 31 + 35? If she ever got free she was 66, the colonies on the eve of Revolution.

Here I must lament discourtesy
this piece of secret history I thought proper to mention

Debtors and criminals met with the like
a *serious hospitality*
of woman's blood   not shed from a wound

Absolute in-fill   drifting page
come to rest on the butt of a gun

In Prince George's County in its first forty years, just twenty-six women convicted, for forty-two births. So, was the law effective? Or was it, from the start, formed in the very image of white fears—that oh-so-famous Irish Nell, who, like a ballad heroine, told Lord Baltimore to his face she would sooner lie with her slave husband, Charles, *than with your Lordship himself*? (Or so they say.)

—
98

Peradventure somewhat difficult
to lengthen a syllable naturally short

hybrid plant   unstable line
of metaphor addicting

if brevet   bribery
braided   bract
kinship   with spaces mended

(someone had to clean up after
throw dry soil over the blood, and sweep)

Not the passion of love, but the act
the act and then   the consequence

Twenty-six women in forty years: fully a third of them bound to Sarah and Sam-
uel Magruder, their heirs, and a few close neighbors with whom they intermar-
ried—the Wilsons, the Willets, the Bowies, the Spriggs. Even fewer women—
only a handful—cleaved to their unacknowledged husbands and repeated the
offense of family. Or, were bred again successfully *by instigation, procurement,
knowledge, permission or contrivance.* Believe what best you like, or most you fear:
most women convicted for multiple births were servants of Magruders and their
kin. Priscilla alone bore seven children, with at least two fathers. For each birth
brought to court and convicted, first by Sary Magruder, *beloved widow* of Samuel;
and then, with great regularity, by William, their son, who it seems inherited
Priscilla along with 193 acres of Turkey Cock Branch, a one-fourth interest in a
Marlborough town lot, and injunction to work for himself from the age of sixteen.
Work, that is, Priscilla's sons, William and Joseph, with sundry slaves unknown.

Word laid down in the desk's clutter
ghost of a sharp, calligraphic style
upturned phallic bud at the branch end

Here, a colored man made his thrust
copied at random, set adrift

'not expect that I shall satisfy'
'and earnestly therefore desire'

(Finlay, the red-haired bard, said this)

1745: a momentous year—how shall we mark it? In Scotland, it was *Bliadhna Theàrlaich*, Charlie's Year, and James Drummond, the Duke of Perth, welcomed Prince Charles to his castle. In the list of rebel officers later indicted, two Alexander McGrouthers—one old, one young—descendants of my Alexander's cousin. Recorded on the male line, with names of mothers optional. In Prince George's County, 26 November: *Priscilla Grimes alias Gray* convicted for the birth of Catherine, her sixth child. For once, the shadow of a father here: a son of Isabella Grimes, another mulatta sentenced at birth to twenty-one years as the property of Sarah Magruder.

Examine threads with a weaver's glass
(irksome path   of the candlelight)
divergent spiral, inturned knot
of forest   at the yett

It's then I go forth for shame's sake
(it is a regular bondage)
traditional mourner, or
a bird
pushed in   to an ecstasy

At Emancipation, slaves named Gray still served in Magruder households, descen-
dants of Priscilla's sons. Who got their freedom at 31. Who left behind their wives
and children—grandchildren—great-grandchildren—as slaves for life. Family fa-
vorites, some of those Grays—promised freedom, named in wills. A long disquisi-
tion on seeming.

Patience in the first line
that none of them be wrested ·
blood-brushing hands   insoluble
For whom am I filling the mirror?

O ten bonny sons I have born unto him
man with one of his legs cocked up
the other turned down toward the line of text

It is of course now impossible
(if filthy quagmire did in earnest put)
prolificke Temperment of Women
provokt by brutal or a fumbling man

if it is a life wound   or seizing the hair of a woman
everything large and everything small
this horizontal kinship, or
blank space with line descending

Then why weep ye for the shambles, for *a' the dreary years sinsyne?* All these *remarkable animadversions* from natural forms made arbitrary: monstrous animals, faces in swarm, vulgate of the curiosities. *A page to discourage the most accomplished.* Hand at left holding a taper. Two left feet at the bottom. Right side trimmed off, a head at the top—but whose? Bells, patens, chalices, altars, law books and prayer books. *New spiral springs an inverted order.* Hounds interlaced like ribbons down the edge of a vellum page. A question mark implies an answer. Surely some error, some breathing place in the middest of verse. *Inure my pen sometimes in that kind. Neither so harde nor so harshe, that it will yeelde.*

then give me, o indulgent fate
sudden ambush   elaborate form
imbedded in *principio*

say *tobacco*   which is to say *the slave*

a gudely gift ye wad gie to me
baritone caress
vibrato
whereby it is to be read or measured

fredome all solace
this ballad book

transshipped from one conveyance to another

Pueblo, Colorado, the central library: a striking new building without enough books to fill it. Waiting for a friend, I wander through half-empty stacks, idly plucking books from the shelves. In a small row of tartan books, travel books, and three copies of *Mary, Queen of Scots*, I'm surprised by Tom Devine's *To the Ends of the Earth: Scotland's Global Diaspora*. On page 37, I read that by 1758, Scottish tobacco imports from Maryland and Virginia exceeded those of London, Bristol, and Liverpool combined, peaking three years later at 47 million pounds sterling—one third of Scottish imports. And what did they do with all that weed? Processed it and turned it around—two-thirds of exports to England and the Continent.

> *I have seven ships all out upon the sea*
> *They are loaded to the brim*

In ballads and broadsides: all those ships, those sailors, those cross-dressing girls: one or two about the slave trade, not one still sung about tobacco. But ships come in and ships go out, and they bring the Demon Lover, with the easiest of all seductions—

> *As they come down through that seaport town*
> *A beautiful ship she did see*
> *Her masts were trimmed with beaten gold*
> *Her spars of ivory*

Months later, I find Tom Devine's facts and figures scribbled on a grocery receipt in my jacket pocket. I'm in Glasgow. It's a bright summer's day. I'm walking on Orinoco Street.

Contest

vb [MF *contester*, fr.L *contestari* to bring
an action at law, fr. *contestari* to call to
witness] *vi* (1603): strive, vie; *vt* (1603) to
make the subject of dispute, contention,
or litigation; dispute, challenge [IE *trei*,
three, II: third person standing by

Call me the patroller of roads
clack of grasshopper in humid thought

Once in a while it helps to pinpoint the error

In penciled relationship   stone house
gravestone in the woods commensurate

to God in a plant   fission or fusion

Capture at night where it roosts
fledged family

(that slight rhythm of fear denotes escape)

Unloved anonymous tutelary
antebellum hurl I want no part of

sloping down to a cool mist

I entered the woods where an old stone wall
(trespass   on my own requirement)

flood water receding, iambic oar
dipped in to the depth of persuasion

Constant escape into other climates
obedience to an unfenced grave

(deceive myself here and be done with it)

1860s: father and sons went west, one died
Brother and two sisters mourned

the loss of their slaves as they saw fit

Deny holograph   trace and scuttle
Kinship remote   commensurate
with debt

*

Now double the absence
refractory than by violent meanes
and not accompted felony

Agrapha   agraphia
adorn aigrette   the hosting

———

Harp notes enclose a sentinel
if graven, grave   if watched, impose
O bloody silence: I

Black knife out of sight to enforce the boundary
absolute unutterable
(one naked figure neighboring)

An army lays a pontoon bridge   an eye surveys the shrubbery
and *Sweet* more than the *Orinoco*

In quartering houses   correction
should induce any man to destroy his own estate

reclaiming   dismembering   discretion
or the better reclaiming the said and deterring others

In dense periphery, trafficke in seed
hated   for my Yankee disease

*

For words not in the index
solander   black umbilicus
sumtyme alarm in fidelitie

Capture the rhythm of fear in a cheap surmise

(she, whatever she
stripping grass seed from its stem)
Between my body and thine

Clan rigor   crest of a wave
suffient to serve very plentifully

black recurrence
sanctum   afetuoso

Their flesh, which is uncommon good

Proscribe

Learn   that words received in childhood
must be carried to the end of the day

proscribe   recite   impetuous
dìteadh gu bàs

Now view of the woods where once was clear

cold hands   wind in your eyes
ruthless proof   of listening

Young I was when first I loved you
teeth whiter than woodbine bloom
lie tonight on half my pallet
cause of my sorrow, etc.

Land   landless

flee with your grammar if you please
do not expect agreement

•

1889, and history begins: Henry Latham Magruder, a lawyer from Chicago, of weak body and sound mind, arrived in Edinburgh to commence research into the origins of Alexander Magruder, Immigrant. Henry was the son of Benjamin Drake Magruder, a justice of Illinois' highest court. Judge Magruder started life in Mississippi, a grandson of the great migration—by which a few planters and a million slaves cleared and settled the southwest frontier. At the time of Secession, young Benjamin moved north—unable to fight the Union, he said, and unwilling to fight the South. His wife was a Yankee from New York State, he himself educated in New England—to which he rode by horseback, so they say, a long month's journey over Indian trails. When Henry set foot in Scotland, though, he was tracing a family journey of another sort

leaves in the forest, one   then two
  foam on the river   meddlesome

this for that   is or isn't

Something made this artificial island

People are apt to become fictitious, Henry wrote, *when talking of their ancestry.* And so, styling himself *no expert* but possessed of a legal and rational mind, he set out in search of actual facts. Alas for Henry, and for us, a fact he took as given was Alexander Magruder's descent from the Clan Gregor, whose virtues, vices, and sufferings formed the root of no less than six published works by Sir Walter Scott—*Wizard of the North*, darling of the South, the man Mark Twain blamed for everything from bad architecture to the Civil War.

—

sweet the blackbird sings his song
sweet the eagle over him
sword in hand   head in the sand
[and mustard seed up the nose will purge the brain]

On the wall of Henry's grandfather's home, as on my parents' and on mine: the Clan Gregor coat of arms and the most famous clan motto: *'S rìoghail mo dhream,* Royal my race. A favorite of the Maryland Magruders, who, like all their landed neighbors, craved *aristocratical* distinction—that fatal peg, on which they and their kind could hang their sense of belatedness, of dispossession, of an unsourced innate nobility transfusing the cruelest temperament with a golden light. They learned that tone from Sir Walter, who made of his Clan Gregor heroes the original Noble Savages, model for Fennimore Cooper, and....but I digress too soon. Just say they were ideal ancestors, those fighting MacGregors, conveniently distant from afternoon haze along the Patuxent, the Mississippi, Chatahoochee, Po. Where planter's sons perfected a *lettered indolence*—land-owning, slave-owning, jealous of honor but short on cash—Romantic heroes stomping plantation dust from their riding boots.

Hence some absurdities are retained
stronghold of harps and a catechism
(audible pain of the plucked string)

But I have nae come tae drink the wine
(the claws correspond exactly)
Come! 'tis the red dawn of the day

—

III

On Clan Gregor history, Henry was as well-informed as could be expected—which is to say he knew from infancy his *Legend of Montrose*, his *Rob Roy*, his *Lady of the Lake,* and had copied out the Clan Gregor entries from Douglas' *Baronage of Scotland*, from tartan books, from *Clans and Septs*. View from the window better than real: despite their noble packaging, all these sources have been described as fiction.

> Kenneth MacAlpin, son of King Alpin
> descended through Dalriadic kings
> from Zedekiah and Solomon
> from Scota, daughter of Pharaoh...

> No, we will not begin there
> It requires instruments we cannot play

So let us leave Henry for the moment, look back at a more corporeal king: that poet-loving, fornicating, *beggarman* James IV—so loved that ten thousand followed him, to die in September, 1513, fighting Henry VIII's army on Flodden Moor. Among them Clan Gregor's feudal master, Sir Duncan Campbell of Glenorchy.

> *but if he had said anarchy*
> irruption soon to run its course

> a sturdy man   a very Knave
> merchant   of perplexity

So this is when the feud blew up—no one knows how—in the years after Flodden. The MacGregors began to flex their muscles, take land they had not been given, revise their genealogy to include a royal footprint, however scuffed, and with it a claim to original rights on land where they long had been *kindly tenants*, including Glen Orchy itself.

> black river first   to distance them
> a fine, shadowy air

But the Glen Orchy Campbells weren't down for the count. In 1550, one Cailean Liath, Grey Colin Campbell, a third son, became the 6th Laird of Glenurquhay when his brothers died. Newly Protestant, a great *improver,* he preferred to *conquess* with imported muscle, evict old neighbors with the stroke of a pen. Proud of his wealth, he commissioned a clerk to inventory his every bucket, saddle, and sword. It was never enough. *Insatiable land fever*—so a Campbell historian says of him—and a deep, mysterious hatred of MacGregors.

> Take count of the guns which the laird has
> of pistolettes, hounds and hagbutts
> of *lokis at the yett and presone dur*
> of great iron fetters for men's feet
> of small iron fetters for men's hands
> of lang chains in the prison high
> of iron wedges, crowbars, nails
> of iron cages, a heading axe
> of gilt harness, of wolf skins
> muskets inlaid with mother-of-pearl
> and evidence of starvation:
> woman convicted at Finlarig
> of bleeding the laird's cattle

                    Or count fether beds
             count Spanish wine and lynnen sheets
        count spynning quheillus, spynnillis, and warping fatts
               count drinking glasses, chandillaris
                 quhyte plaidis and reid mantillis
            brew house, women's house, women's saddles
               wash tubs, candles, tin quart stops
            count keys and kists and hammers and bowls
      little black cups with silver mouths who will you trust?

Now rubble in the inner court, where once *fine musack*, writing games. And Lady
Campbell's famed needlework—the Glenorchy Valances, we call them, mothballed
in a Glasgow museum—one great silk courting of Adam and Eve as they were
expelled from Paradise. Embellished with her own initials and his, joined by a
true-lovers' knot. Though he left poems in the margins of books, children in the
crofts of his estates. *And a great Justiciar all his time.* He planted trees, executed
thieves, *beheddit the laird of M'Gregour himself.*

          how soft dost thou speak   and aimed a blow
               false midnight   of calamity

            He tamed who foolishly aspired
               (aye, every thread of it)

It did not happen all at once, the destruction of Clan Gregor. There were truces, there were calms, intercessions by Queen Mary before she lost her head—Mac-Gregor men comers-and-goers at Finlarig Castle, their presence recorded as an expense: eaters of cheis, harde fische, beir; of Lochtay salmund, auld salt meate, with quhyt whine, claret, *price of the tune*, be careful. For Grey Collin Campbell—who *sustenit thee deidlie feud of the clangregoure ane lang space*—also knew how to bribe and beguile, pick off key men and turn them. *Renounce the laird of M'Gregour and his heirs their chief and choose Colyne Campbell of Glenurquhay and his heirs to be their perpetual chiefs*. With pages of details—of rents and ditches, poultry and kye, of fees and sowing, gude meale and gifts both ways. But most would not turn. And so: letters of amity among friends, sworn bonds to bring their heads in.

> *pleasing to witness hounds pursue*
> (edge-stained, water-stained)
> that old, certain, swift-footed tale

Some of this, maybe all of it, Henry Latham Magruder could have learned, but beyond the edge of this story he dared not look. For Grey Colin Campbell made a lofty marriage—to Katherine Ruthven, one of Lord Ruthven's nine children, eight of whom married to strengthen the Protestant web. Her brother was the next Lord Ruthven, who led the raids of the Protestant Lords. And that leads straight to McGruther country, to Alexander's grandfather, James, put to the horn for *coming with the Protestant lords* against Queen Mary's regiments, at Leith.

hands mingle and alternate
twenty lines of praise, one word crossed out, replaced
calendar notes, the weeks of the year
the measurements of Noah's ark
Subscribed *Invent (?) in bibliam*

then upside-down at torn lower edge
a semi-legible quatrain

So who was his master, this first James McGrudir? David, Lord Drummond. With whom he did battle in a righteous cause. Got outlawed. Got pardoned, 1547. Got his name preserved in ink. Turn another page and what do you find—that Lord Drummond's wife was Lilias Ruthven, eldest of those nine children, making her Grey Colin Campbell's sister-in-law. Go root in the letters, the ones that survive. Or turn the gilt-edged pages of Campbell history. Find Drummond and Campbell in close cahoots, in *mutual Bond of Friendship and Assistance against all oppressors sorners and malefactors*. (Those damn MacGregors still out there somewhere.) Signed at Balloch, 18 August 1589.

now eyes on fire   and altar fire
feet-climb-wet-hell

a *sgian dhu*   black knife
carried by one who crouched in the alphabet

Sorry, Henry, but here's another chapter you dared not parse. 1563: in the background: Queen Mary at bay, and the Catholic clans subjected to Fire and Sword, with special provision for the Glenorchy Campbells to deprive MacGregors of food and drink, weapon and shelter, transport, and care of the sick. 1563: in the foreground: one Margaret McGruder married to one John Drummond, 3rd laird of Drummond-ernoch, cadet to the lords of Strathearn

And on hir he begatt ane sone
ane dochter named and marriet on

Best guess: she might be Alexander's great-aunt. The dates line up, and Drummondearnoch lies near the mouth of Glen Artney, that old McGrouther stomping ground. And in Glen Artney her son, the 4th laird, was a King's Forester—keeper of game—who, in 1586, dared prosecute two poachers. Worse luck for him—*I grieve to have my tale to tell*—the men so used were MacGregors, and their friends had him dragged behind his horse at a gallop through his own forest. Thereafter, his once-handsome head was carried to his sister's house and laid on the dining table. Or was it his hand? No matter: she ran out into a wet night, wild as foxes. Lived rough through that winter, unable to eat from table or stand near fire.

sister, slip through this wire
rattle the bracken   hiss toward light

in document comingled reach
caldera

Maybe. It's fashionable now to say the MacDonalds killed Drummondernoch, the MacGregors mere accomplices. A fat lot of good that does them—the indictment stands, in verse as in Privy Council. *You left handsome John face-down on the moor,* a Gaelic song says of them. *And where is Clan Gregor now?* Clangregoure was *deviled*, put to the horn: McGregor men to be hanged on the spot and pursuers pardoned in advance for murders committed in the chase. *The Earl of Montrose to raise thirty men, my Lord Drummond and his friends forty, and the Laird of Glenurquhay three score.*

> badly written in fresh ink
> or beautifully stained, like a pinto horse
> (a bad direction, worse map
> more guileful than a vengeance)

And thus, and so, and still, and again: when Alexander was in diapers—twenty-three years after the murder and six years after the Proscription —a gang of gentlemen signed yet another bond, at Inchaffray, with familiar names in on the hunt. A young John Drummond of Drummondearnoch, son of the murdered forester; a young Master of Madderty, son of Alexander's father's boss; Alexander's uncle, who farmed at Craigneich; his Drummond half-brother from Belliclone; and another McGruther, an arrowsmith from Glenartney. Does this sound like *McGruder* went hand-in-hand with *MacGregor*? Does this sound like two trails leading back to the same hearth?

Thou sett'ist me to a painful task

> two winds blow through the same wood
> but only one   is whistling

Inchaffray Abbey: now a private house, electronic gate. My friend, never shy, talks our way in, and a shirtless man mowing the lawn introduces himself as the Earl of Inchaffray. With well-bred generosity, he walks us across the flowering grounds to the ruined abbey, declares the remaining masonry sound, invites us to stand on the crown of a vaulted room. From there, we peer through windows in the only wall that survives, at June-green hayfields, rapeseed canary-yellow: fine shades of gray in the black-and-whites my friend later enlarges. We are all drinking beer in the sitting room when the earl's wife comes home. He's showing us some documents from the history of the abbey, or explaining the Royal genealogy of the two Labrador retrievers. *Mother of God,* says his wife, turns her back, pours herself something stronger. Two days later, in Bridge of Allan, a puzzled bookseller hauls out his reference books and we look up the Earl of Inchaffray's title:

> sometimes beneath the heather
> nothing there

2

What's lost might tell a different story
as lostness tells its own story

something I was once   ebullient

by drove road
by caravel
by name

piper in a black sweater
cold country   rain in his hair
such numerous kin and bravery
(to rhyme well enough   with knavery)
riot, rebellion, raid, disorder
we all ways held

a night order
a night forest
(soe many Seduced Anxious Subjects)

It was something my mother told me
something my grandmother promised me

scratch, hide, seek
erase-sketch-bird-invent

I walked a long time   I never arrived
no crossroads

———

Henry Latham Magruder was sure of his ground. As once was I (though curable). Unashamed of what he called the *Magruder cult*, Henry found the Scots *insufficiently informed* on the subject of *American nobility*.

> in strict meter, seat of kings
> (this cabinet   of curiosities)
>
> pen without paper   leaf without tree
> and many streams in the hills

From Alexander to Kenneth mac Alpin, Henry felt sure a line could be drawn— back up the winding road of Clan Gregor chiefs. But the work was exacting, the hours long. So, himself just wishing to *ramble around* the McGruder-MacGregor country, he hired a researcher at the Records House, who quickly announced an unnerving fact: that the name *McGruder*—long thought to have been adopted when *MacGregor* was proscribed—could be found in Strathearn for 150 years before the Proscription. That it played no part at all in the shape-shift from oppressor to oppressed.

> *I am answered   but not aright*
>
> roll of the cannon, beating of drums
> blackthorn   corn sheaves   reddendo

Dashed overnight was the favorite of all Magruder bedtime tales—that a race who had survived in the heather, slept in caves and defied a king, could withstand the rigors of once again losing their patrimony—slaves and houses, wealth and position—so long as their honor, their martial spirit, and Clan Gregor memory, etc.

> *wearily dragging stones along*
> to build this castle wall

> *just like the wheeling mountain winds*
> our wretchedness

Well, you don't claim to be a MacGregor if you give up easily. Henry set himself, and his researcher, to a new and obvious task: finding the bridge—the drove-road, the hand-clasp—between MacGregors and McGruthers. Thus, twenty years later, when Henry's findings came to the attention of Magruders in Maryland and Virginia, hell-bent on founding an American branch of Clan Gregor, he had in his hand the solution: *Gillespie the Cruiter*, third son of a 14th century Clan Gregor chief, Gregor of the Golden Bridles. By Henry's reckoning, this cruitir or harper, bard or seanachie, left a line of sons called by the patronymic, *mac Cruiter*, Son of the Harper, which morphed in the transit from ear to pen into MacCruither, Mac-Crouder, MacGruther, McGruder, to him.

> that out of Original Sacred Tongues
> *parchment rights and dangling wax*
> the work might be hastened, the day turned

3

So where might we look for this Gillespie? Perhaps we'll find his poems and songs in a Clan Gregor castle near Beinn Dòrain, up among the headwaters of Glen Orchy. It's October, 1506, seven years before Flodden, and James IV has dropped in for a week of hunting, entertained in slack hours by MacCailean Mor's harper and one of Glenorchy's bards. MacCailean Mor, by that time, had been by this king created Earl of Argyll and Chancellor of Scotland; and Duncan Campbell, the Laird of Glenorchy, knighted. The MacGregor chief—Ian Dubh of Glenstrae, *who to poets never made refusal*—had led his clan nearly fifty years, in close march with his Campbell overlords. So we can imagine: heroic verse chanted by the Earl's harper; a few panegyrics from Sir Duncan's pet poet; some Latin of course, with a bit of the latest continental verse. And, if the taste of the company ran that way, satires on women to go with the French wines, perhaps recited by Duncan Campbell himself—for he was a prolific and witty poet, as was the Countess of Argyll. Would she have spoken, in the king's presence, her little gem of a poem on her priest's virility?

Writing comes through to reverse side
a nocturnal visitant   alarm!

This was the Northern Renaissance, Highland style. Down in the Lowlands, poets were tuning the Scots language to a perfect pitch. Up at Beinn Dòrain the vernacular was Gaelic, though a bard might recite in Classical Irish, and a well-born lady might understand all three. How do we know? From *The Book of the Dean of Lismore*, a quarto volume, seven inches square, compiled, in the years just after this golden scene, by Seamus and Donnchadh mac Griogair, two curate-poets of Fortingall, at the foot of Glen Lyon.

Counted syllables   o my heart
(rhyme visible in the ash leaves)
hostages without disgrace
when it is blue   and violet blue
above the heavy yellow of the gorse

Horse can't pass this way   or will
heather over broken rock
thirty-one miles of stumbling
night   and day

Now loch hides under the reservoir
no edge intact   a coastline
written on but much rubbed:
lady's name encoded in the names of trees
young man with beautiful hair
famous elopements   magical plaid
covers no woman who has been untrue

[read it out to the bard you got it from
endure his jokes, correct it]

with bardic markings   crossed and strayed
committing devastations

Copying error   slash marks
exempted by   no stream so swift
as leaves in windy weather

Song Book of the Pillagers, one of its poems calls it. Languages tumble and mix in its pages like a Highland stream rushing toward the gentler straths—Gaelic sounds in a Scots spelling, Irish poems in a Roman hand; Ossianic chants, the tales of Fionn; religious tracts, praises, elegies; with pieces *more or less indecent*, satires, laments, and aphorisms. Imported paper, expensive ink, beautiful columns of matching words—all taken down from memory or the recitation of poets: aristocrats sure of an audience, cultivating their metropolitan tastes; local scribes penning verses between less lofty tasks; *chief's bards*—well-kept, lacerating each other with very fine blades; and strolling bards—mere *pack men*—who were *apt to arrive at evening, followed close by their hounds.* By the time Seamus and Duncan MacGregor were making their book, the world it recorded had all but vanished, dismembered by new-fangled forms of greed; by death; by feud; by the Reformation; war.

> *taste its fruit when it was red*
> mounted female in a hunting scene
> *not historical, but history-like*
> dark-stained and mountainous pages

> Capitals used indiscriminately
> C & T tend to be interchangeable   how droll
> Lost in the perished edge of the leaf
> the incerthanging strophic forms
> of hero on a bloody bier

> *Then praised be this Gregorach!*
> *praised in ancient forms with a straight tongue!*
> (unlikely, sir, it's a delicacy
> or blade, not meant for children)

So where in this mix do we find Gillespie? Not mentioned by Seamus MacGregor, the Dean of Lismore—curate, notary, poet, and man of letters—favored by Campbell appointment and promotion, as his fathers had been for a hundred years. Nor by his brother, Duncan, one of the book's most accomplished poets. Nor by Finlay, the Red-Haired Bard, whose poems beg favor from the Clan Gregor chief, Ian Dubh—that *white-toothed falcon of the three glens*, whose sword hand, blue eyes, wife, and wine all gather praise. Not to mention Ian Dubh's horse—a fleet dun, whose metrical gallop, translators say, resembles the flight of swallows.

> *might of the brightness, might of the storm*
> and all wrought withering

No, the Dean's Book figures not in Henry's persuasions. He could have seen it, must have seen it, in Scotland if not at home, in its 1862 translation—with a four-beat meter to woo our Englished ears. But if Henry saw it, he never said so. Nor, in writing of Gillespie, did he cite any evidence stronger than *it is my belief*—a phrase quickly altered, by those who came after, to *it is traditional, it is said*. Said that Gilawnene MacCrouder, who signed his name, 1447, was Gillespie the Cruiter's son. Induced, perhaps, by Campbell expansion to seek patronage in the Drummond desmesne? Or maybe Gillespie went off in a huff, when the Glenorchy Campbells gave the Chancellery of Fortingall to the Dean of Lismore's great-grandfather, ordaining *him* their chosen man of letters. You can make a story, if it's story you want. (God knows I've tried.) But here's the rub: linguists say McGruther / MacGrowther / MacCrowder / McGruder doesn't derive from *Cruitir*, but from *Grùdair*, brewer—a skill much cultivated in great monasteries like Dull—though how they know, in that throng of spellings, I cannot say. *Remote connection from a common stock*—those were Henry's words, in a letter urging his fellow Magruders not to take *MacGregor* too literally.

O reddish bracken, golden broom
tattoo *MacGregor* across your ribs
(with other stray marks once meaningful)

now fit to paper   wind persuade
and who owe   fidelity

On the internet now, from time to time, someone suggests Magruders should be wearing Drummond tartan. You can't fault the logic, but where's the fun? For Drummonds, surviving meant keeping your head in the dark alleyways of court politics. Are there Drummond laments? Beheadings? A single pipe tune celebrating homicide? (Well, maybe there's one, that 14th c. incident, when they burned down a church full of Murrays . . .)

No, you won't catch me cashing in my counterfeit MacGregors for a Sterling issue of Drummond, with that lawyery motto: *Gang warily*. Much better Clan Gregor's shout: *E'en do and spare nocht!*—which translates, roughly, as *Damn the torpedoes, full speed ahead.*

apology for my treachery
which ever can be tested by rime

one hand, two inks   a scorch mark
footprint of the storm   in an hourglass

4

So Magruders continued to romp as they willed. To say Alexander had changed his name. To say his brother, James McGruder of Cargill, was recognized as Chief of Clan Gregor—after all the men in the main branch were hanged, beheaded, shot, burned, or banished. To put on their spectacles, clear their throats, and hold forth for a good half hour on Grimm's Law, a purely phonetic transmogrification of a nobleman's factor from Strathearn to an outlawed Highlander nobler than those who hunted him. *First g has coalesced with k, while the tongue-tip stop-d takes the place of the second g. And as to the vowels, closing r has a* marked vocal murmur, *as in friar, speaker, nadir, author, sulfur, satyr,* thus: *MacGregor, Makriger, Macgrugir, Magruder*—

> topography authentic   disarranged
> (rough words must be subdued with use)
> *and failing to interpret, writes*

> bad genealogy   worse verse
> one whole story filled with stone

Henry must have consulted a linguist. How else come up with that old word, *cruit*, or the Irish *cruitir*? What seems to us shaky and unlikely must have felt to him like a solid path, a paving stone found ten feet under the soil. Starry-eyed as any, he dreamed of buying a Maryland plantation, dubbing it *Castle Magruder*. For this, we can certainly blame Sir Walter Scott, whose influence ran to *sham castles* as well as sham genealogies, the cult of chivalry, jousting matches—and of course antiquarians, dabbling in heraldry, rimes and relics, anything *scattered in ruins.*

success of Nobleheartedness
in hawkynge, huntynge, a ready fist
(my muse hath made a willfully lye)
of two double-bridles, plow points
plow shoe and stocking garters
log chain, black pepper, silk threat
(I meant *thread*)
one barrel of tar and trim the hedges
a fee for sharpening scythes

But Sir Walter was not quite Henry's excuse. Only half a *Southron*, and raised on
the open side of the South's intellectual blockade, he might have read Dickens as
well as Scott. Might have quoted Shelley, even Emerson, along with Burns and
Byron and Carlyle. No, *his* problem was his great-grandfather, Captain James Tru-
man Magruder, who retired from the sea to marry and farm. Who carried a paint-
ing of the Clan Gregor coat of arms all the way from Maryland to the Mississippi
frontier. Who said he got it in Aberdeen, a gift from his kinsman, Alexander John
William Oliphant MacGregor, *alias* Drummond, 6th of Balhaldie, who in 1714 was
elected chief of Clan Gregor by fourteen surviving, though *semi-ruined* men.

examine threads with a weaver's glass
noble the blood, rare the shore
that is or isn't   seannachie

Aback the tongue
infill of wish

within this acre of rubble hides the spark

And they were related how, exactly? Henry Latham does not say. He says it all happened in 1800, by which time this particular MacGregor of Balhaldie was six years dead. When Balhaldie died, in the West Indies, James Truman Magruder was twenty-six, and already long at sea. He's said to have sailed round the planet twice, seen Paris during the Terror, captained a merchant ship out of Philadelphia. His ship logs survive—some of them—but record no voyage to Aberdeen. Balhaldie's son—in case we'd like to cast him for this part—lived most of his life in the Indies. He styled himself Chief in the 1790s, but Clan Gregor preferred a chief in residence, and elected another.

> Stand at a window set in a wall
> that now connects to nothing
>
> workmanship creates a view
> small tree stiff in wind
> crest of the wave rising

The coat of arms passed down in the family at least till 1909, when Henry Latham Magruder was corresponding with kinsmen dead set on founding a clan society—whether *Clan Gregor* or solely *Magruder* not quite decided. *Risk the ridiculous, height of folly*—those are Henry's words I've underlined—for a handful of Magruder men to speak *for the whole surname of MacGregor in America*. But the die seemed cast when one embellished Henry's story, describing the coat of arms as belonging, in particular, to the *Magruder branch* of Clan Gregor.

> upright cross imposed on a circle
> sparkle of mica in the stone
>
> 'what harm' 'why not' 'including thee'
> *And down the fitful breeze thy numbers fling*

———

131

So, is Henry's story true? MacGregor of Balhaldie, the elder, was born in France to an exiled Jacobite family, but raised by his mother's people at Inchbraikie, not five miles from Inchaffray. He was there long enough to know McGruthers, if he didn't know them in his Perthshire regiment, or among the exiled Drummonds in Paris. Whatever the story, wherever they met, whatever Balhaldie believed or said, James Truman Magruder spent six years farming in Prince George's County before he lit out for the southwest frontier. Long enough to spread the contagion. And who in the *knightly class* of the county would spurn such Romantic origins? In 1820, by a special act of the Maryland legislature, John Smith Magruder, great-great grandson of Sarah and Samuel, changed his children's name to *McGregor,* for

it is impossible to sing in prose

Yet why did it matter, Henry asked, if Alexander Magruder was a member of Clan Gregor, or merely a branch from its distant root? *Undubitably a Highland mac,* the Magruder name had a 250-year history here, while the name MacGregor had none. *Magruder Federation,* he suggested, or even *Clan Magruder.* But what did *he* know? A man of far more pen than sword. Not *born to the habit of command.* Unlikely to fence, ride, dance, or hunt. A connoisseur neither of horses nor of hounds. His letters bear a Northern postmark: what need did *he* have of *Clan Gregor who show no fear*? Of *who can tell me where they have gone*?

O hear, thou Chief of the Gael
take from me the real serpent
leave the abstract sign

Flowers step up the ruined walls
(with great iron fetters for men's feet
with small iron fetters for men's hands)

> Bang it out bravely   boil your salt
> a higher mathematics of   consent

For the men Henry was arguing with, *an outlawed and imperishable name* gave luster to the Lost Cause. *Fifty darkeys our willing slaves,* wrote one in a sentimental moment, the whole of childhood silhouetted and stilled. *Indeed we were born with castles in mind, and brought up accordingly.* Scottish tutors, exiled for their Jacobite leanings. French dancing-masters, exiled for their blue blood. Graffito of the memory. Make welcome, m'lord, an history.

> Then give me, O indulgent fate
> Gaeltacht   in beautiful border
> whole space of the body regulated
> encircle   what am I   hridder

> Tail of the beast terminates in leaf
> half-uncial and interlace
> an unnatural drawing:
> literate five hundred years

> Yet how travel this *via sancte*
> moving word
> where I step down the path becomes a house

> *Wine, wax, honey, song*
> Agitating these matters in my mind

> *It's queer how I dream of the old slave cabins*
> *standing again*
> *and marvelously enlarged*

In Purpose at My Booke

In waking, or   in narrow pass
circumscribe · reset
we   who came for a witness

Elaborate from the territory
inner map of resistance   daily drawn

lost in the perished edge of the leaf

Or drinking wine in the stone fortress
stronghold of harps   of obduracy

Took me, carry me   some forty miles

if brevet   bribery
braided   bract

less terrifying distances
pretended   and adjoined

Walking on ice as if on land
economic incentive   or

Difficult   is sanctuary

1795: Great-great grandson, Ninian
self-reliance led to the breaking
came into this wilderness
no log to serve as drag
took family across Ashby's Gap
graveyard behind the garden, he
purchased
built
cut
developed
married
fathered
had
a wife and numerous slaves

grist mill *was built*
saw mill *was built*
distillery adjoining

dimensions of   and a water spout
journey a difficulty, but

mammy slave and a second wife

barn *was built*
milk house *was built*
kitchen *was built*
school house *was built*
torn down

This is what you might call *passive construction*
verbs lost in wild   grammar enslaved
dropped comma on the black coast
a syntax of periphery

"Ninian built his dwelling house"

39 lashes
and salt the wounds
mill carriage run by a rag wheel
which children had to tread

1795: *And though it be a shame to us to tell it,* Maryland was a divided state, the border not beside it but within. In the north and west: slavery competed with immigration, industry, and the labor of free men, black and white. In the south: half the population enslaved. The other half: rich planters and poor planters, few free tradesmen, no middle class. Younger sons immigrated west, to the Maryland Piedmont or the far Shenandoah, *unplanted by any man.* At the peak of migration, one quarter of slaves carried inland to new homesteads, clearing woods and breaking sod for those who later would claim those mountains as the natural home of free men.

Pleasing to witness hounds pursue
(that old, certain, swift-footed tale)

bodye for bodye   who would tell
the scarecrow   or the fire

Three hundred a year made good their escape, but most weren't running to freedom: they were running home. For even those not parted, were parted: half of all masters owned fewer than three. Marriage possible only to neighbors. Who stayed neighbors. So family, still, a *complicated flaw*: pipe airs of love or lamentation, whistled at the window, and an *unprecedented network of roads* webbing plantations together like spider silk.

I asked where that road leads   what road
raveled clue   of the syllable

I was brave the day we parted
but I had an arrow in my side

footpath through a damaged wall
land that rises   and rises up

spinners and knitters   stockings and gloves
heavy cloth from the mill   the washing

(housemaid stood ready with peacock plumes
to keep flies off the table)

no stoves, but particular
to have their dresses just touch the ground all round

Ann, a brown girl
Linny, the housemaid
my cook, Jane
Black Margaret

And the laws, the laws   oure rude language
all inured   to the difficulty

if sumtyme *be scanned in both lines as it is scanned in line five*
(antithesis to clarify   abominable night)

It was the loan of you that broke me
child off-center   ghost of him
between my legs   or all of it

vine-killed sapling in winter woods
sack of corn on a horse   small boy on top
straight road, good luck, two miles

limit of   and out of hearing

Beating my fists on the ground

2

1808: the importation of slaves abolished, and a new cash crop for the Chesapeake: young slaves to be sold south, to clear and plant Jefferson's new frontier. And die there by the thousands.

> edge-stained, water-stained
> (launching boats on the little stream)
> apples rot in a bed of nettles
> limbs   into a labyrinth

As always, though, more than one story, and more than one point on the compass. In Prince George's County, planters had another market for their excess slaves: they could hire them out—to merchants, hotels, and builders in Washington City; or to blacksmiths, bricklayers, ship riggers, sea captains and carpenters in the booming port city of Baltimore. To be sold south was a kind of death. To be hired north, perhaps a life. In the sprawl of warehouses, workshops, docks, forges and mills, you could work beside free men and women. You could learn their demeanor, learn to pass as free. Or bargain with a master for your own hire. Counter the threat of sale with the threat of running. With a white woman on your family tree, you might even petition for freedom, tie up the master's time and money, and tie his hands at the auction block—a tactic that sometimes resulted in jubilee.

> patience in the first lyne
> grammar of descent   intransigent
>
> And yet   a pocket pistol

a likely, bright, Mulatto lad
a swaggering walk and very black
pretends to have an uncle, calls her his wife
to St. Mary's County, where he was born
called Dick, but calls himself Richard Wallace
supposed he is concealed by friends
has a free husband, has a quick step
to Carroll County, where he was bought
to Roderick McGregor's, where her husband lives
proud in his carriage   his back is scarred
a good Cooper and Carpenter
and has at many times changed her name
five foot seven, five foot two
has twice before made his escape
with upwards of forty scars on his back
a jobber, a sailor, a cook, a maid
and knows horses very well
he is fond of talk, a great Rogue
and a man who passes for his father
took with him a fiddle, a bonja, some cloaths
absconded from the Northampton Furnace
ran away from the Lancaster works
was last employed on the South River
his working clothes, his tools, his hat
quick-spoken and artful, a joiner by trade
trained as a waiter, a pastry cook
has a scar in the palm of his right hand
took a bay mare and an old saddle
all masters of vessels are hereby forewarned

———

can read and write, will pass as free
as sawyer, ship-caulker, and waterman
a good house servant and useful groom
a dark mulatto with light eyes
a likely stout fellow but rather loose made
has lived in Annapolis, Lancaster, Baltimore
sailed two years to the Eastern shore
a remarkable mimic, a ship-rigger
a pert, palavering wench of middle size
understands plastering and white-washing
brought up to bricklaying and rope making
a good second hand in the baking business
and when drunk stammers in his speech
there is hardly any thing in a common way
but what he understands and can do
professes something of the shoemaker's trade
my cook, my coachman, my seamstress, my maid
took with her a mulatto child
my yellow wench named Hannah
my negro man named Glasgow

And what thou lovest well remains

3

At Anchovae Hills, 1798: 231 acres remaining. Dwelling house in such bad repair that George, son of Nathaniel, and his wife Sarah, maiden name unknown, wintered in their tobacco barn. Labored in the fields beside their slaves. Prepared for ruin. George dead before the century turned. So in 1805, this *other* Sarah Magruder freed her slaves—or thus they called it. Each one named in her last will—their *use and benefit* passed on—to one beloved grandson, for a term.

Now count how many hours in the year

My negro man named London for one year and a half, thereafter to have his freedom, his house and its furniture. That 10-foot house, in poor repair. *One negro boy named Henson, until he shall arrive to the age of thirty.* His age at the writing of her will unknown. *One negro named Saba the term of seven years, and to the aforesaid Saba all my coarse wearing clothes such are made in the family*—by slaves. *Her children, if any, born in that time, to serve to the age of thirty.* Freedom itself defined by bondage: copious, pithie, significative. Black families split among free and enslaved—enslaved for life, to a certain age, to a year.

O dae ye see yon high, high hills
The sun shines on sae brawly?
They are a' mine and shall be thine

gilt cleath soiled   unmannerly

Ah yes, the peril of widows, and of all who owned little of value except their slaves. With no overseer, no cash to pay a slave-catcher, no way to make a living without the faithful service of those with little reason to be faithful. Forge, plantation, rope-works, hotel: it made no difference. Without slave labor the place would go bust, and the slaves knew it. So make them *safe property,* give them a stake in it, give them a reason not to run, or shirk, or slit your throat. Always a good behavior clause—with *faithlessness* and *malingering* solely defined by the master. A weak promise, but such as it was it might prevent flight at the time of a master's death, guarantee labor to the heirs for a certain term. And not to worry: there were years of work to extract first, from a strong back or a skilled hand, before the joyful day. And years of childbearing, and childrearing—to feed Maryland's *other* export crop.

> *Now sit every man in the readiest place*
> (seanachie at the door of the feasting house)
>
> in faint trace of negation   smoke
> to coil a body barely
>
> (slash marks to divide the words
> neglected for their lack of euphemism)
>
> Looking glass, bookcase, two desks, looking glass
> tea table, twelve chairs, andirions, looking glass
> two black mares and a Chickasaw colt
>
> *One man negro*   named

A term slave wasn't worth much, in cash, and couldn't be sold across state lines; so the deal made a kind of insurance—so long as the mistress kept her word, the master didn't go bankrupt, the heirs didn't turn to the courts to undo the will. Slaves couldn't testify, couldn't sue, couldn't enter into a contract, couldn't force the master or mistress to record a deed of promised manumission, making it irrevocable. But they could work badly, and they could run, and they did, *with as much inconvenience as could be expected*. Since 1790, Baltimore printers had offered an interested master or dame boilerplate forms for manumission, with blank spaces left for the name, the age, and the date of freedom. *For diverse good causes and considerations*. In light of the love and affection I have for [him] [her]. As well as the sum of [   ] dollars. *Provided that the said negroes shall serve faithful and in all things*. Including production of new, young slaves, whose children and grandchildren could provide the heirs with bound labor for fifty years, eighty... you count them. Families thus might be bound to each other—black and white, free and enslaved—till long after the key was lost. *Ink very black, one can hardly resist*. On pathways spiraling round and down, filled in, crossed out, corrected. To search for other parts of their bodies. Nearly concealed or passing into.

'turn under path'   'meet the lover'
children hereafter to bee borne
in stasis   of perplexity

One meeter of verse be answerable
suffer itself to be controlled by a passion

Sarah Magruder, 4 slaves. James Magruder, 26 slaves. Susannah Magruder, 13 slaves. Negro Terry, free. Henry Collins, free mulatto. Polly Carter, free mulatto. Doctor Henry, free negro. John Magruder, 25 slaves. Henry, free negro. Tom, free negro. Mary Magruder, 14 slaves. Verlinda, Ned. John Adams, free negro. Thomas Magruder, 11 slaves. Dennis Magruder, 47 slaves. John Smith, free negro. Samuel Easton, free negro. Peter Gray, free negro. Kate, Rachel. William Magruder, 45 slaves. John R. Magruder, 58 slaves. Ab^m Williams, free negro. George Wedge, free mulatto. Philip, free negro. Lotty Boteler, free negro. Cupid, free negro. Richard Gray, free negro. Thomas Gray, free negro. Charles Graham, free negro. Milly Gray, free negro. Francis Magruder, 26 slaves. Lancaster [illegible], free negro. Thomas Barton, free negro. Eddie Jackson, free negro. Benjamin Gray, free negro. Alexander Magruder, no slaves. Thomas Magruder, 3 slaves. Isaac Magruder, 6 slaves. Samuel Magruder, 5 slaves. Hannah. Bob. Cupid Plume, free negro.

Prince George's County, 1800, 3rd District, *Perpetuity*

So, who was Sarah Magruder's fourth slave? The mother of Henson? Dead, sold, or free by 1805? And was his father a free man of that name, one of the oldest free black names in the county? *Household* is only edifice. Behind its shield, slaves are *difficult to say*. Attribution migrates through three centuries of women, a figure concealed by intricate path. If I durst come into her company, possess without knowing, *quho coud wele endyte*: conveyor and herself conveyed: how many limbs redrawn into the labyrinth? Women with children: the husband and father invisible, enslaved. Black farmers with property, black farmers without: fewer than half with free wives. White farmer, unmarried, his mulatto son: slave mother forever out of kingdom's reach. Listed elsewhere by sex and age: but body had she, body did she, durable goods on a Slave Schedule. How many chosen? How many chose? *A streak of milk on one cheek, streak of blood on the other.* Blurred name on a deed of manumission. Something my mother told me.

it was in the archives I learned to hunt
from far away the intimate

three thousand cards in the census files
thirty-three lines in the phone book
one mailbox on a mountain road

how travel this
via sancte

scroll of microfilm over a single heart

4

Handsome, black-eyed Captain Jack. More properly, John Smith Magruder, a great-great grandson of Samuel and Sarah Magruder of Good Luck. Born 1767, in time for the Revolution. Died 1825, tail-end of the Jeffersonian world. He served in a Scots Militia, 1814, Prince George's County. Wore his title with romantic swagger: both the luck and the swagger part of his patrimony. His grandfather, John Magruder of Dunblane, once gambled away the family home-place—an event camouflaged in Magruder history under the heading *bon vivant*. John's tough-minded wife, Susannah Smith, got the property back, made him sign everything over to their oldest sons—slaves, plantations, and businesses. Captain Jack's father got a profitable store, and more. Passed on to Jack a nice plump 2100 acres. No record survives of how the executors divvied up the slaves, whose given names we can read in the inventory: Harry, a blacksmith, 45; Clare, 32, with a 3-month child; Ben, Tom, Molly, Cupit, Charles . . . eighteen in all, with seven of them under ten, a kind of *futures trading* for Jack and his sibs.

Such rude and undigested papers
old plantations of the new world

Gaelic notes in the margin   every wind
the one I have elected and must serve

Dashing, doubting Captain Jack. Who read Scott's novels to his children at night, at his dwelling place, Grampian Hills. Who named two sons for their grandfathers—Henry and Nathaniel—but all the rest for the heroes of Romantic tales: Mortimer, from *Children of the Abbey*; Alaric, *last of the Goths*; Roderick, for Scott's bold Hielandman, Roderick Dhu; and Ellen, the *Lady of the Lake*. They were heady days in the county. James Truman Magruder was home from the sea, toting that Clan Gregor coat-of-arms, telling his tales. He and hundreds of others getting ready to abandon Maryland's tobacco-depleted soils for the far southwest: Louisiana, Mississippi, Kentucky. Come 1814, the slaves were restless, the Brits sailing gunships up the creeks, burning the old warehouse at Magruder's Landing. Militia called out, slowing the redcoats—though not much—on their way to burn Washington City. August 24: the conflagration. August 25: *the blackest morning I ever saw*, as tornadoes unroofed barns and leveled tobacco houses all over the county.

In the golden book of leaden gods
a boy vidette   a yellow stain
And how now to the battery

To cross or to circle apparently
To cross or to circle or sink or to stratify
with path internalized
an arranged ballast

Roll of the cannon, beating of drums
such *dreadfully realistic days*

Jack's wife, Eleanor, was a Clarke widow but a Hall by birth. In 1817, her unmarried brother wrote his will, left land and stock and two young slaves to Dolly Mullen and her son Henry, mulattos. Freed 27 of his 33 slaves, most of them family to Dolly and Henry, and to men and women working in Eleanor's own house: cooking, cleaning, sewing, and raising the kids. Jack himself had a vision—or so his daughter told *her* granddaughter—after which he converted from French philosophers to God. Was it before or after he married? Was it before or after he petitioned the legislature to change the surname of his children to *McGregor*?

> Thus fallen to me in pleasant places
> a hill among trees   a lost stone
> of which transcribe   the riddle

> *To hear her sing the old Scottish songs*

> On a rise of land above the landing
> feral flowers where a house had been

> Son of the Harper, seannachie
> explains the agitation

> *A Maryland pine is my clan badge*
> *and a cow's tail my coat of arms*

> though gilt with the initials of a king

1825: Captain Jack dead. The second son, Roderick, just 21 and already in debt, a racer of horses and a generous host, taking over the family plantations. 1826: Jefferson dead, and the intellectual mood shifting, bumped hard to the right by the cotton gin, which spread the profits of slave labor to the mills of New England, Glasgow, Lancaster, Liverpool. 1831: Nat Turner's Rebellion fed white fears, while the launch of *The Liberator* drew a new line in the public sands. And, in the Virginia Assembly, the last debate about slavery on southern soil.

For our wordes can not well bee forced
to abyde the touch of Position

Incised letters where earth collects
grave slab   with alphabet of moss

Read now with fingertips   an unbearable softness

1831, December: Roderick McGregor married Ann Eleanor Eversfield Berry, widow Eaton, descended through her grandmother from Sarah and Samuel Magruder of Good Luck. 1832: Ann's older brother, Elisha Berry, a man *of dissipated habits,* came into his inheritance and had a new house built on Springfield, his plantation. Left his wife and kids in the big house, moved to the new one with a slave woman, Eliza. No record to say if she consented. No definition of *consent*. Lived there nine years, till his fortunes were ruined and his white children grown. 1841: his son-in-law got possession of Eliza, tricked her, with her children, into a D.C. slave pen—sold to James Burch, a slave trader.

Scholars lift this heavy page
goatskin   illuminated
where *cumal* means a female slave   or coin

Dare interpret   dare apprentice, say
grotesque human form in clasp of a dragon, or
obviously a Holy Figure
same size but plainer, fainter

muddy plaiding   spin and spinner
now browderit with satine   heavy axe
to ghost the mimic houses

In New Orleans, Eliza and Randall, her son, were sold for fieldwork, different
masters. The daughter, Emily—7 or 8 years old, with *admirable beauty*, light skin
and long curls—not sold, but held, to be groomed and raised for the sex trade.
How do we know? Because Solomon Northup, a free man kidnapped on a D.C.
street—drugged, chained, robbed, and sold to James Burch in April of 1841—was
literate. He wrote her story along with his own, *on feet made tender by smallpox,*
all the way to her death on a Delta cotton plantation.

I spoke aloud a neckerchief
a muslin neckerchief, ruffled or plain
but the sound of my voice startled me

black-forsaken-alphabet
red gore   of the childbed

Oh yes   these
punctilios of genealogy

Say difficult without it, say
to publish scarifies   creates

Lord of Misrule to maintain the order

Prince George's County, the 1850 Census, household #554 in the Marlborough
District: Roderick McGregor, 44, white male in *household* of one. Plus 35 slaves,
estate of $22,715. He looks like a bachelor, or widower, but we find his wife, Ann,
two pages away, in Household #452, with her mother. #451: her younger brother.
#453: Dick Brown, a mulatto man freed by Ann's grandfather four years before she
was born. And next to him, #454, Ann's sister-in-law, wife of Roderick's brother
Henry, living with a free mulatto family headed by William Wedge—descendant
of a slave named Daniel, and of Mary Wedge, a white servant woman convicted in
1727 for mulatto bastardy. Her first of five. Sold to her master, Thomas Harwood,
whose descendants intermarried with Berrys for a hundred years.

Be it kent by all men   of the jewells and silver
the kye young and old and the wild mares
honor, not conscience
shame, not guilt
word mislaid in the desk's clutter

by other names   recklessness
an ink but slightly darker than the page

Inchaffray   Anchovrie   Dunblane   Good Luck

by brank or brandy
bruise or break

this heart-shaped design made of spirals

Item: ane fair silver brotch sett with precious stones

where *dàn* can mean a poem   or fate

come to rest on a woman's skin

5

1851: Anchovie Hills indentured, divided: 30 acres, 50, 100, *all that part east of the main branch thereafter*. Abolition illegal, by state constitutional reform, and the soil desperate, growing that *stinking weed*. Deeds of partition. Seizures for debt. 1857, at Grampian Hills: Roderick McGregor, like his father, dead before the age of 60. Manumitted by will: one William Bowie and his wife Matilda, with three of their children. Set up with a house, a horse, a cart, and some cash, in Washington City. But where were the rest? A grown son first run away, then caught, saved from being sold south by a sympathetic neighbor. Another son: found in draft records of the Union Army. And daughters, scattered east and south, not reunited for thirty years. And where was Ann McGregor? Not in Roderick's will, and not in his house. 1843: she had purchased from her mother their home plantation, Berry's Grove, and would there outlive her husband by twenty years. (Cohabitation? His or hers? A quarrel after the sale of Eliza? Or over her family's habit of faking bankruptcy to escape their debts? And which of them kept the 59 slaves inherited from her grandmother? I don't know, no records say, don't ask me.)

> Do hereby bequeath to my said nephew
> Elisha E. Berry
> all my slave or negro property
> held, owned and possessed
> at the time the said   were emancipated
> all profits or moneys that may hereafter
> accrue from or be paid for
> or any other manner whatsoever   this

And to Enoch Burgess, colored
for long and faithful, etc.
4 acres & a cow
with house to be built by my said executor
not to exceed $100
not to exceed

blackthorn   corn sheeves

this cup of healing far from clear
horrifying tenancy   of ebb

1858: manumission made illegal in Maryland, but with already a free population nearly as large as that enslaved, the two intermarried, inter-layered: seek them in the pages of a century of laws. Requiring free blacks to leave the state, to hire out where told, to *apprentice* their children by age four. Declaring them—like the 16th and 17th century displaced English poor—*vagrant* if they refused. Sentencing vagrants to bondage. Forbidding blacks from trafficking—in bacon, pork, beef, mutton, corn, wheat, tobacco, rye or oats. Couldn't own guns or booze or dogs. Couldn't operate boats. Couldn't read, though half did. And could be sold, if the person who had freed them went bankrupt. 1858: attempts to re-enslave them—75,000 free men and women—to define them as abandoned property, subject to seizure—just as a cart, abandoned on a public roadway, would devolve upon authorities for safe disposal. Laws against gypsies. Laws against whistling. *Tinted freedom in somber shade.* This devilish difficulty. Of *liquidating slave property* without creating freed slaves.

If I hesitate, it comes to meet
earthed syllable   bad footing here
in distance from the moment to the word
accent depressed or snatchèd up
into immoderate fantasy

One *lampe of licht*   indigenous
defeated once, it reappears
as weapon

Household #555: Ellen Henson, free black ser-
vant, literate. Household #556: Ann & Wm
Wedge, mulattos, literate. Household #454: Eli-
za McGregor, 40 years, in household with Wm
& S.T. Wedge, three generations, free mulat-
tos, literate. Household #1184: Peter & Matilda
Magruder, free Negroes, trade unknown, 60
and 65 years old, literate. He, freed in the last
ten years. She, by birth a Henson. Household
#1182: Henson Magruder, black man, 20, liter-
ate. Household #90: C. Magruder, black woman,
servant in a merchant's house, 30 years old, liter-
ate. Household #96, Second Series, A. Maguder,
free black man, 45 years old, 2 children and his
wife, Mary Bowling, literate. Household #95:
Andrew Magruder and his wife H., literate.

Literate meant: *able to write one's name*

Clem, my blacksmith
Nanny, my servant
my capenter, Old Basil,
& Ester Mullen his wife
my carpenter, Young Basil
and Sukey, his wife
William Bowie & Matilda his wife
with three of their children—not Junior, not Jack
for $20 frees Susan Dodson
for $280 sells Joseph Mullen to Basil Mullen
sells Dolly Mullen to Basil Mullen
sells Deborah Digges to Basil Mullen
frees George Gray, William Gray, Silvester
Manuel, Henry, and Susan Dodson
Richard, James & Charity
to serve 18 years and then be free
serve 32 years and then be free
Lucy Gray, Toby Gray
youngest child of the said Lucy
George Gray, Bill Gray, William Woods
Josephine and Josephine's children
Martha and (two lines later) Martha's children
frees Lewis Taylor, frees Sam Gantt
one half of a house to Sam & George
one half to the children of M & J
frees Frederick Taylor
frees Thomas Nichols
no further mention and no provision
for *Alexander, my negro boy*

1861: by accident, *contiguity to free states*, Maryland became *an ambiguous ally of Union*. 1864: Emancipation, passed by a petulant State Assembly. *And o god the shame of it*. Not even a stump to stand on, and the dollar's rash exactitude: land without labor: worth less than a good cow. 1867: Judge Daniel Randall Magruder, another of Samuel and Sarah's tribe, indicted by the Freedman's Bureau for sentencing black prisoners, without trial, to term slavery on Maryland farms. A *privilege withheld from whites*, wrote the governor in Magruder's defense. For theft of a one-dollar pocket-book, a three-dollar pig, a five-dollar beehive, a $25 lot of tobacco: rotting corpse of slavery exhumed—*clarsach, corbel, a human head*—and freedom of this world a trifle *compared with when the Cross shall maketh free*.

Night journey on foot   gospel commences
asymmetrically disposed
by clan rigor, intricate path
nearly concealed or passing into
white hood lined with plaidie

Woe to the wretch who fails to rear
At this dread sign   eternity
salt trafficke   twisted path
of rethorike that found the flouris faire

To my sons and daughters, Negroes

black verger   passive voice
That his deeds may be made manifest
take name of him who enslaved you

Then prove ye Ruin of a Country
crows in the oak and a loud excursion
one hawk hunched in a pine

Almost the center of all direction
vulgar idiom   a bit
of worm that ate ships' hulls

Not a Southern state, my mother said
—just an X between two stanzas—

unarrived, unknown, unnamed
And violent waves shattering

A placeing of them   where it is pretended
sawn asunder, tempted, slain

or *suddenly from an ambuscade*

condensed to scattered footprints   walls
rectangular   a script

In the first law of Heaven and Earth
there is no such thing as a noncombatant

Vault center   bats at dusk

If the dog barks again, wake me

Baltimore, 1967, the annual gathering of the American Clan Gregor Society, flawed only by the unpracticed hands of office staff called in to serve the Saturday banquet—climax of the weekend, evening dress only—when the regular wait-staff go on strike. My father, who will later remind me of this night, assumes it's a union problem, but doesn't ask. He's not a Magruder, though married to one, and holds no sway. Jump to 1976, and my father, handsome in his new kilt, has been running the Gathering for four years. In the cocktail hour before the banquet, he's checking details, admiring the centerpieces, the flags, and the large banner of the Fiery Cross, hung, as always, behind the head table. But there's a wee problem. The wait-staff, all black, refuse to work in the banquet hall so long as that banner is there. My father asks to speak to them, and with (I am sure) great charm and tact, explains the history of the Fiery Cross, its legendary use as a symbol to call the clan to arms—men running picturesquely over the heather, house to house and glen to glen, carrying hand-sized pitch-pine torches in the shape of a double-armed cross. See? It's there on the banquet program, too, above a few lines from Sir Walter Scott. Nothing at all to do with the KKK. He is sure of this, and sure that his explanation has put their minds at ease. Nevertheless, he takes down the banner, mentions it to no one; and neither at the banquet nor afterwards does anyone remark on its absence. My father runs the Gatherings for more than twenty years, and the banner is never seen again.

6

NIGHT orders are not good and these were mine: ane sword and oak tree crossit beneath ane crowne. Hounds interlace like ribbons down the edge of an empty page, whose absent figure shapes the tale. Bedtime story, hero of first. O water-crossing, water wide, who can measure, who *sail o'er* such froward, couthie, lawless, vast dis-levelment?

> *then build me a boat that can carry two*
> provocateur   or provenance
> my ink-black ship   disquietude
> my now quaint similitude

> *For a' the blood that's shed on earth*
> *Runs through the springs o thát countríe*

> cluster of huts   in a wilding marked
> for beggarte and extinction

> in ballad method, wayward wood
> internal refrain   or wakening

> *His metir swete, he maketh joy—*

> Difficult is sanctuary

•

> [cannot write beautiful lines here
> presence   odd hurdle

———

twenty lines of attempt and a cheap knife
my tutor missplls to protect the Name
cut margins   discoloration
intersect the spaces

contradiction from which an exit becomes
space above pillars   the very place

rest   escape   immaculate
intermarried in me

All endit was my innocence
for whiche though I in purpose at my booke

Literate means   *I can write this name*
any contract so signed is binding

•

then how track   past prurient

through bays of darkening   and sleep
a laced ecstatic green of shallow seas

ink net   where once desire
rifted by   refugium

that only one's own body can be possessed

Black Magruder, wash this verb

in clan rigor   crest of a wave
      vagility   unattested

still to go upon the hethe
a swallow's turn   turns in mid-air
            to heft

And it's I will do for my love's sake
What many a lady will not do

Ink very black, this waukrife hour
Disturbance of commodity

With fornication   genuine death
uppon a quiet company of words

Transport

n (1611) **1**: an act or process of transport-
ing **2**: a strong often intensely pleasurable
emotion **3**: a vehicle used to transport per-
sons or goods **4**: a transported prisoner

This could be a mad woman followed by explosions: billboards, antennae, ce-
ment. In a shopping cart the ruined ground condenses to accusation: a diet of
pavement, entire continent mapped in elephant skin. Begun, this only elaborates:
elegant crosshatch of timber in an old tobacco barn. Alexander, the leaf I stole
was half as long as my arm. It smelled like a penitentiary. I inhaled, repented, a
thousand times before breakfast. Still, in the cemetery, thirty-eight skeletons lie
in sixteen graves. Outside the fence, eleven stones sullen. Oaks persuade. Garru-
lous pines speak a cheekbone. I make a face for you: flight of pelicans, low, over
brown water. Skin type becomes catastrophe, a form of beach erosion, neurologi-
cal pathway of a text: *Lawful to trafficke.*

Alexander, when I write your name, the letters rise over their words like bare masts on a caravel. Their ropes divorce adversity, pass through multiplied dangers, seeking me. Today it is winter, and light falls into oak with the same logic: it seeks capture: rival gesture. *I was walking in woods and came on a cemetery. Someone had cut the dead grass, so green could rush out tenderly to light--*

Rubrisher of the Origin, approve this labor. By vines and flowers, seed-pods, webs, snake skins, and dead field spiders. Otherwise I must illuminate for myself the true gravity: beginning at *A,* undertaking voyage. Someone had cut weed trees in the fenceline, restored the view. Of passing cars, defend the faith, etc. Everything I know arrived with you, ratline coiled in returning vowels, quarterdeck raised on the outstretched arm of r. Oh, Guide Letter, Sovereign, seize this landscape, thy espoused impenetrate: that the work might be hastened, the soil turned, habitation written into arrival. No verb after hesitation.

The place is a plaine ground, growne over wth trees and undershrubs without passage. I opened a cattail there: it boiled out like lava and flew. I can please myself that easily, or, I can make a gathering: blackbirds on the rushes, the word *imprimus*: *All my wearing clothes and my Great Bible.* Alexander, this is to warn you: I smelled the hope you left and was not destroyed. I opened your will and found it there, misspelled like the name of a woman thrown into the sea. She was named *Witch*, but the windes did not thus remitt their violence. They took on the force of an acorn: one hundred women exported and sold, for marriage and plantation. Yours not the one miscarried. At her first shore, a paleographic footprint: staghorn, detritus, a disinhabited shell. *Fifty acres for this conception:* upright cross superimposed on a circle.

Oh dread incorporate.

To take oneself, via plantation. I opened a cattail: *heirs of her body lawfully conceived.* Bravura of the black skin. Not risk Maroon. A paving.

On ivory-handled carving knives, geese fly open-mouthed away from flesh. This I inherited at the moment Mattapanient was preserved, coiled into a text of feasting. No reason to feign innocence: I study them, I study you. Their habit of gathering bones, and yours of intercepting them. No reason to conceal your lack of interest in their fate: among your own, a death-feast, bounty for the rest. I undertake this carving up, this parceling. I scratch into you an epigraph, and into them design. There's a place on the river where 98 ducks fell dead in the mouths of two men—we were able to count them—and a landing where what could be sold coagulated, for a certain fee. It was how you lived. At the place they lived, Alexander, foundations circle immanence; absent walls entertain calamity. I possess both, and for a certain fee will display them anywhere. This is my trophy room, this text of repentance. When I lift your knife, my palm obscures spent bone. I become your preservation, antique in my veins, like a metal cooled from eruption.

In this passage through flesh I am laying up stores. In heaven, they say: standing above the captive face of meat.

Alexander, I tried to escape you, but you have made good on the family promise: survive, come back, gather by night where the day is dangerous. Your animal has tracked me down, your signal fire ignites in my eyes when I close them, I come when you call, back over a continent not fully mine, all the way down to the landing that bears your name: there a woman half black, half Indian, coughs into her hand an idea, and I have to watch, I have to take it from her as I took from my mother milk. Do you understand? I can name the stars, the ship, body parts of a horse, plantations misspelled into place on the ruins of Indian towns. But I am only allowed one name and I have to choose it, I have to go in, lie down, in the morning look out, say *fox squirrel, house finch, white-tailed deer,* imagine that this is inhabitation, the face a sediment laced with bone, blade: look, I can dig that up as well as you, I can hum the begats, I keep a museum, shelves: of beheadings, thefts, babies delivered at sword-point into snow: I descend from them all, a miracle: twelve thousand of us testify in twenty-one spellings, the name broken up like a ship: vines near the shore, winter: tree limbs like broken rigging run by rats.

There: I've said it: in rat middens thirty thousand years old, scientists read our history: this is ecstasy: *you* magnified to the size of a finger bone.

Alexander, the gravestones vibrate in traffic noise. I leaned against them, and struggled to hold oblivion. Held. In my womb no sound. Rock and blood on the verge of partition. Land voice without responsory. What is left of the oak trees layered. And I, relict of the voyaging, refraction at point of displacement— placed--there, in deciduous certainty. Something appears. A many. Oak branches moved but silently, the road quantifying. I leaned, Alexander, I did not embrace. Stones outside the fence were not contracted: to aftermost light and the sanctuary. Survival by pleasing: I did not say on which stone. Grave, ruin, foundation, fence: consult in order to disregard. I am civil dissent, unproved acres; you are commerce of persuasion. What feast enjoyed in speculate, as the singer drags her hair across the syphilitic bones of a slave.

Dread voice. Disobedient thou. Red thread from an ossuary.

I wanted to bury myself, but the poor old castle had fallen down.

The horse came closer just now, I can hear him breathing, I can see starlight on the barbed wire, so can he. He's looking for an animal who could be you, looking for flash of fox, or a mallard's wing: you are something else, a fence maybe, and the fox goes under and the horse keeps away, so as never to admit he's not free, and by then it's full dark, August dark, the moon's not up, so a deer coming down to water inhabits only its sound and becomes a bear: forget about fear: it lives here, it isn't you. Come morning I'll walk up the road, looking: you don't wear shoes anymore, your tracks might be what's left when I pick up nails. Alexander, you know how this feels, how a voyage expects to arrive. You knew when the bow opened sea through ten thousand geese you had seen God, were doomed. *Here's faith,* you said, and began to draw longitudinal lines on the cattails, bug-dry in August: the animal who could have been you was a cottontail rabbit, whose nest you crushed pulling stumps in an Indian cornfield. It was what you could do: take three wives, open up a new plantation every seven years, write a learnéd treatise on exhaustion. This is what I can do: define *hogshead,* find the landing place, stop smoking.

I am reading this poem to a dead oak: it turns out there must be two to receive the spirit: the one to speak and the one to understand.

Alexander I opened your will I know what you left me. Something compressed as a cattail, accurate as a falcon's wing. *That as soone as it shall please god they shall arrive.* Manufactures accounted fair. Fenceline elaborated: to strip mall. I know there is an oath required to receive. Write my name to contain the narrative. A single, in the architecture of perishing. Yet how to inscribe inconsequence: thirty-four verbs for murder: sea clap, and I have been there. *Ten foot diameter; two towers, one round, one square. Before the invention of chimneys. Two rooms for armed men, closed yard, a heading pit.* In the woods now, who cleared? In the woods now, who farmed the periphery? *Slue a wilde Boare, who was fast upon them. Unearthed a young oak to shield his king.* Awarded in lexicon:

Oh   my   chevalier

Out of snow to the fifty acres. Out of death to the expedient. Ten thousand geese in the estuary. Who is it? Who speaks to my dreaming, says, *in regard the land is goode?* I am holding an acorn. I swear by that. And the 7–11 gleams on the edge of an anvil, heated to light.

This is a blow, my genitor—my bright—my battering. I blacken myself in the transitive. Alexander, I am seeking to love you.

Notes

Anent • **1** *Coir' a' claidheamh* (COR a CHLYuv) GAELIC: right of the sword. **1** *Reddendum* SCOTS: feudal rent, paid in kind. **1** *Fause knicht* SCOTS: false knight, Child Ballad #3: The False Knight Upon the Road, an encounter between the Devil and a child. **2** *"While there's leaves in the forest and foam on the river, / MacGregor, despite them, shall flourish forever!"*: Sir Walter Scott, refrain of "MacGregor's Gathering." **2** *Seanachie, shanachie, seanchaidh* (SHENuchy) GAELIC: reciter of tales, historian, bard. **2** *Ri* SCOTS LATIN: King. **2** Phyllomorphic: leaf shaped, or a changeable leaf shape. **3** *'S rìoghail mo dhream* (is-REEghal mo ghraym) GAELIC: royal my blood, commonly translated as "my race is royal."

& Anent • **5** *Then will ye tak the gun the gun . . .* : The Dowie Dens o Yarrow, Child Ballad #214.

Night Orders • **6** *Night orders are not good:* a Highland proverb. **6** *Ane sword and oak tree . . .*: coat of arms of the chief of Clan Gregor. **6** *Ri Albain*: a list of the kings of Alban/Scotland. **6** *Martyrdom red, white, or green*: in the Celtic church: death, exile, or hermitage. **6** *St. Adomnán's Law* (ADomnan) IRISH: a 9th c. Gaelic document, now claimed as the first law in heaven and earth for protection of noncombatants. **7** *Garron* SCOTS: a small highland horse. **7** *Get ye doun frae ma horse . . .* : The Fair Flower of Northumberland, an elopement gone wrong, Child Ballad #9. **8** *Child with a streak of milk . . .* : Adomnán's Law. **8** *Thirl* SCOTS: pierce, thrill, vibrate, pass through; also enslave, bind, enthrall. **11** *Spreigh, spreach* (spree) SCOTS: raid, plunder, wreckage, originally a herd of stolen cattle. **12** *Sturt* SCOTS: conflict, trouble, violence. **12** *Hanged on a black, blasphemous cross*: the execution of Alaisdair MacGregor, Chief of Clan Gregor, 1604, nine months after the Proscription. **13** *McTarlich, MhicTheàrlach* (MacCHYARluch) GAELIC. **13** *Craig* SCOTS, from Gaelic *creag* (crayk): crag * *Gnoc* (CHRAWchk) GAELIC: knock, hillock * *Coire* (CAWruh) GAELIC: lit. "kettle": a hollow on the side of a hill (in Scots: *corrie*) * *Weem* SCOTS: cave. **14** *To putt down innosent men...*: testimony of Alaisdair MacGregor to the Privy Council. **16** *Griogal Cridhe* (GREEgal CREEuh)

GAELIC: more properly "Cumha Ghriogair MhicGhriogair Ghlinn Sreith/Lament for Gregor MacGregor of Glenstrae," attributed to Marion Campbell, his wife (1570). **18** *Puir pepelis* SCOTS: poor people. **19** *Then what's the blood . . . my hawk:* My Son David, a fratricide ballad, Child #13. **20** *Herskit* SCOTS: bitter grief and trouble, heartbreak.

Meadow ◆ **23** *That noe Contest may arise...*: codicil of Alexander Magruder's will. **23** *Landing places for goods:* the meaning of *Potomac*. **23** *As dies in hissing gore the spark*: Sir Walter Scott, "The Fiery Cross of Clan Alpin."

In Peace of Warres ◆ **25** *Skaith* SCOTS: damage, hurt, trespass. **29** *Widowed land*: Francis Jennings' description of the North America discovered by European adventurers: a land already swept by epidemics of European diseases. **30** *Murtherers*: small cannon. **35** *Storms Brewed in Other Men's Worlds,* by Elizabeth A. H. John, is among the few books of contact history that embrace the full complexity of the subject, including European political contexts and Native agency. **35** *Tuilzie* (TOOLye) SCOTS: a quarrel, a brawl, a dust-up. **36** *Trowes* MIDDLE ENGLISH: Think, believe. **40** *Now sit every man in the readiest place*: traditional invocation by a seannachie about to perform. **40** *Graithed* SCOTS: clothed, armored, dressed, harnessed.

Old-Fields ◆ **42** *In shirts and Drawers...*: Ebenezer Cook, "The Sot-Weed Factor" (1708). **42** *That stincking weed of America*: King James VI & I, who famously hated tobacco. **43** *Sweet* & *Orinoco*: varieties of tobacco. **44** *To be extirpit and ruitit out*: from the Proscription of Clan Gregor, 1603.

Heath ◆ **50** *Sasine* SCOTS: transfer of feudal land rights. **50** *A bairn's part of gear*: a child's portion of inheritance. **51** *Hership*: hardship, destitution, caused by *harrying* or acts of violence. **53** *To luif him weill and do him na skaith* SCOTS: To love him well and do him no hurt. **54** *Banqueting House to the scaffold*: route of Charles I to his execution. **60** One of *Glen Lyon's goddesses* is Cailleach, still honored by the tending of iconic river stones. **61** *Abdhaine* (ABthanu), obsolete in Gaelic, though it survives in Irish. **62** *Gille Eonain* (GEELuh YOHNain) GAELIC. **62** *Grùdair* (GROOdair) GAELIC: brewer. **65** *Beggarman ballads:* Child #279 & 280:

———

The Beggarman, The Gaberlunzie Man. **66** *Lang heff I maed of ladyes quhyt . . .* *tar barrel, etc.*: "Of Ane Blak-Moir," William Dunbar (16th c.): Long have I made [written] of ladies white / Now of a black I will write.

In the Stranger's Land ◆ **75** *In the stranger's land are plenty of wealth and wailing*: translation of a line in "Stór Mo Chroí," an Irish emigration song. **78** *She's bound his wound with a golden rod*: Archie Fisher, "Witch of the West-Mer-land."

Hairst ◆ **82** *Retoured*: in Scottish law: returned, as in "returned a verdict." **85** *He that ay has livyt fre*: John Barbour, *The Bruce* (14th c.): He that always has lived free. **86** *Ryvir* SCOTS: reiver, raider. **86** *Delyverit* SCOTS: delivered. **86** *Ourgilt / owrgilt* SCOTS: gilded. **86** *I that in heill wes and gladnes*: William Dunbar, "Lament for the Makaris [Makers]" (16th c.) SCOTS: I that in health was and gladness. **86** *Doolie* SCOTS: doleful; as a noun a *doolie* is a ghost or spectre. **89** *Osnaburg, Osnabrig* (and many other spellings): a coarse linen used for sacking and for slaves' clothing; originally from Osnabrück, Germany. **95** *I leaned my back unto an oak . . .*: a floater verse, always associated with a lover's betrayal; in The Cruel Mother, Child #20, a betrayed woman braces herself against the tree to deliver her father-less child. **95** *That God in all his werkis wittie is*: Robert Henryson, "The Preiching of the Swallow" (15th c.). **97** Mynglet SCOTS: mingled. **100** *Bliadhna Theàrlaich* (BLEEaghna CHYARluch) GAELIC. **100** Yett SCOTS: gate. **102** *If it is a life wound . . .* Adomnán's Law. **104** *I have seven ships . . .*: Fair Annie, Child #62. **104** *As they come down through that seaport town . . .*: The Demon Lover, Child #243.

Contest ◆ **106** *1860s: father and sons went west . . .*: my great-great grandfather, Fielder Montgomery Magruder, & his sons & daughters, most of whom never mar-ried and never left the family farm in Prince George's County.

Proscribe ◆ **109** *Dìteadh gu bàs* (JEETuh goo baa) GAELIC: condemnation unto death, from the Proscription of Clan Gregor, 1603. **110** *Artificial islands* were built by early Celtic monks as dysarts, places of solitude. **111** *Clan Gregor coat of arms*: a coat of arms belongs not to the clan but to its chief, and should not be displayed by anyone else; but you're wasting your breath on Americans trying to explain that. **111** *Aristocratical*: one of several peculiarly southern usages adopted from the writings of Sir Walter Scott. **111** *Come! 'tis the red dawn of the day*: "Maryland, My Maryland" (1861), composed by James J. Randall, a white Marylander exiled in Louisiana. **113** *Kindly tenants*: families who had occupied the land since before the tenure of its feudal overlord. **113** *Liath* (LEEuh) GAELIC: grey. **113** *Take count of the guns . . . mother-of pearl; Feather beds . . . silver mouths*: Inventories of Breadalbane (16th c.). **113** *Bleeding the laird's cattle*: in starving times, people survived on cow's blood, sometimes mixed with milk. **116** *Sgian dhu* (SKEEun doo) GAELIC: lit. "black knife," a concealed knife, often worn in a stocking. **125.** *Languages tumble and mix . . .* Though Gaelic was the Highland vernacular, 16th c. letters among Highland noblemen and women were penned in Scots, the language of government, in an orthography known as *secretary hand*. The Book of the Dean of Lismore's texts employ the same orthography, and its Gaelic is spelled according to Scots phonetics. **131** *And down the fitful breeze thy numbers flung*: Sir Walter Scott, first stanza of *The Lady of the Lake,* before the stag is chased up Glen Artney. **133** *Fifty darkeys our willing slaves*: Edward May Magruder, a founder of the American Clan Gregor Society. **133** Indeed *we were born with castles in mind* & *It's queer how I dream . . . marvelously enlarged*: Alice Maude Ewell, granddaughter of Ellen McGregor Ewell, Roderick McGregor's sister. **133** *Gaeltacht, Gaidhealtachd* (GEHLtucht, GEHLaltuchk): the Gaelic people, Gaelic world. **133** *Hridder* OLD ENGLISH: sieve, riddle.

In Purpose at My Booke ◆ **142** *O dae ye see yon high, high hills . . .*: promised to the Collier Laddie's lover, if she'll give him up and marry a rich man. **142** *Cleath* SCOTS: cloth. **144** *Turn under path, Meet the lover*: symbols used by Gaelic scribes to indicate that the following phrase should be read at the end of the next full line. **149** *A Maryland pine . . . coat of arms*: attributed to John Smith Magruder (Captain Jack) by his great-granddaughter, Alice Maude Ewell. **152** *Kye* SCOTS: cattle. **153** *Dàn* (daan) GAELIC. **158** *Woe to the wretch who fails to rear / At this dread sign the ready spear!*: Sir Walter Scott, "The Fiery Cross of Clan Alpin," from *The Lady of the Lake*. **161** *Couthie* SCOTS: comfortable, snug, agreeable; from *couth*: known. **161** *Then build me a boat that can carry two*: The Water Is Wide, traditional. **161** *For a' the blood that's shed on earth . . .*: Thomas Rhymer, Child #37: a sojourn in the elvish lands, as guest of the elvish queen. **162** In Gaelic usage, *only one's own body can be possessed*. Grammatically, not even hunger or fear can be owned. **163**

And it's I will do for my love's sake…: Clerk Sanders, Child #69: a woman's vow of chastity and deprivation, after her lover has been murdered by her brothers. **163** *Waukrife* scots: wakeful, unsleeping, restless.

Transport ◆ **166** *Rubrisher:* illuminator. **166** *Guide letter:* a small letter entered in the space left for an illiterate rubrisher, to be sure he drew the correct letter. **167** *Maroon:* a slave who rebelled and lived free. **168** *Mattapanient:* a native town excavated in southern Maryland. **170** *Relict:* widow.

Visit Traffickeblog.com.

Acknowledgments

The writing of *Trafficke* has been supported by many friends and by the kindness of strangers. Those who helped with sources include Phebe Jacobsen, retired archivist for the State of Maryland; Wayne Clark, archaeologist at Jefferson Paterson Museum Park; folklorist Margaret Yocom; historians Martin MacGregor, Lesley Smith, and the late John Hemphill; and staff members at the National Library of Scotland, Edinburgh Central Library, Innerpeffray Library, the Maryland Hall of Records, and the Lansdale Library Special Collections at the University of Baltimore. Special thanks to Maoilios Caimbeul for his help with the Gaelic. Mistakes are undoubtedly mine.

For help and hospitality in Scotland, I would like to thank Don McGruther for years of researching the family story, plus one lovely outing in Strathearn; Hugh & Margie Rose in Glen Artney; Margaret Bennett in Comrie; Alec Finlay in Edinburgh; Ian Whyte at Inchaffray Abbey; Mr. and Mrs. Ian Ritchie at Belliclone Farm; and Neil Hooper in Glen Lyon. On the home front, Sue Emerson has done Herculean work in the hunt for Alexander's descendants. Jill Magruder Gatwood and the African American Magruder Facebook group have been inspirational, as has James Louis Bacon, a descendant of William and Matilda Bowie. I also thank George Mason University for two Creative Awards in support of travel and research.

To those who critiqued its various drafts and excursions: *Trafficke* would have been a poor traveler without you. I thank especially its early readers—Allison Cobb, Jennifer Coleman, Caroline Hemphill, and Peter Streckfus—and those who helped clean it up for public consumption—Martha Collins, Danika Myers, Lesley Smith, Margaret Yocom, and Tracy Zeman. To all who have rambled with me in McGruder / McGregor country: here's to the pleasure of old roads.

And, finally, deepest gratitude to Janet Holmes.

About the Author

SUSAN TICHY is the author of *Gallowglass* (Ahsahta, 2010), *Bone Pagoda* (Ahsahta, 2007), *A Smell of Burning Starts the Day*, and *The Hands in Exile*, a National Poetry Series title. Her poems, collaborations, and mixed-genre works have been widely published in the U.S. and Britain, and have been recognized by numerous awards. She teaches in the MFA and BFA programs at George Mason University, and when not teaching lives in a ghost town in the southern Colorado Rockies. She is a member of Coming to the Table, a non-profit organization that provides leadership, resources, and a supportive environment for all who wish to acknowledge and heal the wounds from racism rooted in the United States' history of slavery.

AHSAHTA PRESS

SAWTOOTH POETRY PRIZE SERIES

2002: Aaron McCollough, *Welkin* (Brenda Hillman, judge)

2003: Graham Foust, *Leave the Room to Itself* (Joe Wenderoth, judge)

2004: Noah Eli Gordon, *The Area of Sound Called the Subtone* (Claudia Rankine, judge)

2005: Karla Kelsey, *Knowledge, Forms, The Aviary* (Carolyn Forché, judge)

2006: Paige Ackerson-Kiely, *In No One's Land* (D. A. Powell, judge)

2007: Rusty Morrison, *the true keeps calm biding its story* (Peter Gizzi, judge)

2008: Barbara Maloutas, *the whole Marie* (C. D. Wright, judge)

2009: Julie Carr, *100 Notes on Violence* (Rae Armantrout, judge)

2010: James Meetze, *Dayglo* (Terrance Hayes, judge)

2011: Karen Rigby, *Chinoiserie* (Paul Hoover, judge)

2012: T. Zachary Cotler, *Sonnets to the Humans* (Heather McHugh, judge)

2013: David Bartone, *Practice on Mountains* (Dan Beachy-Quick, judge)

2014: Aaron Apps, *Dear Herculine* (Mei-mei Berssenbrugge, judge)

AHSAHTA PRESS

NEW SERIES

This book is set in Apollo MT type
with Garamond Premier Pro titles
by Ahsahta Press at Boise State University.
Cover design by Quemadura.
Book design by Janet Holmes.

AHSAHTA PRESS

2015

JANET HOLMES, DIRECTOR

ADRIAN KIEN, ASSISTANT DIRECTOR

DENISE BICKFORD

KATIE FULLER

LAURA ROGHAAR

ELIZABETH SMITH

KERRI WEBSTER